The Romeo Club

The Romeo Club

RESTLESS OLD MEN EATING OUT

Vincent Graziano

In loving memory of AnnMarie and Oliver

Also by Vincent Graziano

Die Laughing

The Family Jewels

Prologue

Late afternoon, the Tuesday after Super Bowl LII, in 2018, Frankie Grace stood outside Johnny Paradise's Italian Restaurant and examined the pattern of bullets that had, a day earlier, shattered the palladium glass window, nearly killing Tim Collins, one of his best friends. Glaziers were working to replace the glass, removing jagged pieces from the frame, as busboys swept thousands of shards from the scene. The neon sign left dangling in the open space, "Welcome to Paradise," seemed comically out of place. He looked to the spot where he'd found Tim in the bushes. At that moment, he thought Tim was dead. It had all happened so quickly—the shooting, the sirens, the police, the ambulance. He remembered picking up Tim's phone and seeing the last caller. As Frankie looked at the wall now, something did not sit well with him. He wasn't buying the theory that the events of that afternoon amounted to a botched hit on mafia chieftain Sam Napoli, who had been eating in the restaurant. But what did he know? He was an undertaker, not a detective. Still, he was curious and wondered, *Who is Sergi, the last caller on Tim's phone?* He turned to his other friends Johnny and Nino Paradise, and Dr. Cardio, who were watching him. "Something is wrong," he said.

Chapter I

On the Friday before that Super Bowl, Tim Collins sat behind his desk in his office. Beyond a glass partition was his staff, some busy at workstations, others hustling back and forth trying to look busy. His bookkeeper was jockeying from file cabinet to file cabinet, providing requested information to an auditor from New York State Department of Taxation. The auditor was a diminutive man, with male-pattern baldness and oily skin that caused his glasses to continuously slide down his nose. He'd been parked in the outer office going on three weeks. Coincidentally, another auditor from the IRS, more buttoned-down, slick hair, and professional looking, was also going through spreadsheets at a desk provided for him. Neither would be a welcome lunch guest.

Timmy Collins turned his attention to a more-pressing problem. On the computer screen before him, Draft Kings, an online gambling site, laid out all the statistics and information about Sunday's Super Bowl LII. His desk was covered with material regarding the match-up between Tom Brady, leading the New England Patriots, against the Philadelphia Eagles, with some neophyte, Nick Foles, taking the snap. A backup quarterback to boot. Foles against Brady, who'd be going for his sixth ring. Collins meticulously compared players to players, positions to positions, stats, figures, and percentages. He studied the injury list, the unknowns, putting it all together in his foolproof system that had proved invaluable in limiting his losses over the football season. When all his calculations and figurations were finished, he took a coin from his pocket and tossed it into the air. That was confirmation enough. He picked up the phone, dialed, and spoke, "This is Timmy C. New England ten dimes." A voice on the other end acknowledged—"Covered"—and then *Click*. He made four other calls placing the same bet. At the same time, he jiggled his computer mouse in his fingers, watching the corresponding arrow dance on the screen. He brought the arrow to "Proceed" and pressed. The circular icon spun as the Draft Kings validated his credit card. Legal betting was fine and certainly convenient but a bit antiseptic and unfulfilling. There was something missing for him. The allure of the back room, the phone calls, the meetings with connected men added to the adrenaline rush, not to mention the tax implications. The excitement and intrigue could not be duplicated with legal sites. That is why he still kept the local bookies busy. Timmy was hopeful. His fantasy team had been more of a nightmare this year, but he had faith in his system. Besides, his selection had been verified by the coin toss. He waited for confirmation; instead he saw the word "Declined." Two other credit cards had the same result. The third one worked. That one belonged to his wife, Tracy. He made three other phone calls to place bets as he cursed the conspiracy against him by Visa, Mastercard, and American Express. His local bookies weren't so particular about credit ratings or delinquent payments.

He opened a drawer and looked into a vanity mirror, adjusting his hairpiece. The jet-black wig sat like a dead cat on his head, and the sides contrasted sharply with the remaining gray hair that encircled his head like a friar's. Then he took an envelope containing $5,000 in cash from his desk drawer. He owed it and more due to a slight aberration in his system. The envelope was short what was needed to satisfy the debt, but he was sure that, by Monday, he'd be in good graces again. Music sang out from beneath the pile of papers on his desk: Sinatra's "Fly Me to the Moon," the definitive rendition, according to Timmy. He found the phone and declined the call. He put an unlit cigar between his teeth, put the envelope into his pocket, and walked into the outer office humming the tune.

His bookkeeper was biting her nails. She stole glances at him; her jaw clicked as she adjusted her dentures. He stared down the oily auditor, who did not return his gaze. "I'm going to lunch," he announced. The fed looked up at the clock on the wall. Eleven a.m.

"Mr. Collins, can I ask for a day off on Monday?" the bookkeeper asked.

The jaw thing was annoying. "Sally, can you ask me when I get back from lunch?"

Her lips turned down. Her jaw clicked. "But . . . sometimes you don't get back from lunch," she whispered.

Mmmm, she has a point. "Okay. Okay, sure. Take Monday."

Tim stepped out onto the avenue. His office was in the heart of Inlet Cove, a small bedroom community in Westchester County, north of Manhattan. Cafés, restaurants, and pizzerias surrounded him. He walked with the swagger of a politician leading a parade, offering a jovial wave to countless pedestrians along the way. Some shouted, "Hey, Timmy, how goes it?" Tim Collins was a fixture in this town. He stopped at a cigar bar a few blocks from his office. The air was thick with smoke. Men were bellied up to the bar, drinking booze and coughing up phlegm. Large-screen televisions flashed sportscasters from all over the world. Analysts over-analyzed every aspect of the upcoming game.

Laws prohibiting smoking in restaurants had given birth to this new "cigar bar" phenomenon. It was a loophole that allowed smoking and drinking without a liquor license. Find a storefront, call it a private club, charge a yearly fee to join, bring your own liquor, and so much for smoking ordinances and liquor laws. Necessity is the mother of invention. Large exhaust fans hummed in the background in a futile effort to purify the air.

Timmy worked his way through the haze toward the back room, fist-bumping friends and acquaintances along the way. A barmaid in a spandex bodysuit rubbed against him. "Hi, Timmy. You didn't call me last night."

"Sweetheart, sweetheart, I'm a married man." He winked and patted her backside. "Is he in?"

She tilted her head toward the back room. She wiggled her cell phone in front of his face, mouthing *Call me*.

He found who he was looking for in his usual place, feet up on a desk. Five o'clock shadow at 11 a.m. Tim pulled the envelope from his pocket and tossed it on the desk.

The man looked up. "It looks light. Feels light, too," he said, weighing it in his hand.

"It's half. I need a few days," Tim answered.

"Timmy boy, Timmy boy. What am I gonna do with you?"

"Just a few days," Tim said again.

The man rubbed his palms together and cracked his knuckles. "I'll pass the message along. It's not my call. He's upset. You don't answer calls. Word is we're not the only ones waiting for you to settle up."

"Rumors," Tim said. "I'll see you Monday."

"Why don't you stay? He'll be here shortly. You can tell him yourself. Better that way."

"I'm meeting friends for lunch, or I would. See you Monday."

Tim high-fived his way out of the cigar bar, declining the offers for a quick one.

❋

Chapter II

Johnny Paradise was sitting on a high-back stool behind the bar fingering through receipts. It wasn't pretty. As owner for twenty years of the restaurant that bore his name, he'd seen a steady decline in business over the last five. The restaurant was situated on the neglected side of the Metro-North Railroad near the New York-Connecticut border. Like everything else on this side of the tracks of Inlet Cove, it had seen better days. Businesses left, taking with them the lunch crowd. Day laborers ate lunch from paper bags. It was all reflected in the numbers. Johnny put the receipts in a box and scratched his head. He took a small comb from his pocket and ran it across his perfectly trimmed walrus mustache.

The neighborhood consisted of light-manufacturing plants, sprinkled among illegal three-family homes with worn vinyl siding and aluminum gutters tearing away from the fascia. Air conditioners clung tenaciously to rotted wooden window jambs. It was a work-ing-class community, with more cars than garage space and more landscape trucks than lawns, overflow-parked and double-parked along narrow streets with competing potholes. Locals changed oil and spark plugs in their driveways. Side yards were graveyards for tire-less, late-model Fords rusting on cinder blocks.

Most businesses had closed or relocated, leaving behind those that didn't have the option. Muffler and brake repair, tool and dye, fence, drywall, and lumber mills remained, fighting to stay alive in the shadow of the insatiable Home Depot, lurking like Godzilla in a Japanese movie, ready to attack and destroy all who stood in its way. It was only a matter of time. The beast would be fed.

Paradise's Italian Restaurant was now the jewel in this hybrid neighborhood, a free-standing building situated between a commercial chain-link-fence company and an auto-detailing shop. The blinking neon sign in the large window beckoning, "*Welcome to Paradise*" added a touch of irony amid the urban decay. Patrons were leery about spending time in this part of town, even with the common knowledge that they'd be safe at Johnny Paradise's Italian Restaurant. Johnny was connected to the right people.

The restaurant was a relic from bygone days. Thick red-velvet drapes hung over the entrance doors, blocking cold wind gusts from knocking menus and assorted business flyers off the maître d's podium. The drapes stayed up through summer, trapping whatever cool air blew from a groaning compressor. Checkered red-and-white tablecloths, straw-covered Chianti bottles, and a jukebox with a myriad of musical choices, as long as they were sung by Sinatra. Eddie Howard and D. Rose singing "Happy Birthday" with a flourish of "For He's a Jolly Good Fellow" also made the cut—always a hit when performed by a quartet of Ecuadorian waiters and busboys. There was a vase with a somewhat wilted flower on each table, the flowers courtesy of the Grace Funeral Home. Johnny insisted on the most recent. There was a tin-hammered ceiling and sawdust under the floorboards behind the bar. Except for the commissioned portrait of Johnny's father hanging above the cash register, all the other artwork might well have been paint-by-number: generic, faded, clumpy pastels of the Bay of Naples, a garden Sorrento, a seascape of Positano, and the inevitable table with cheese and grapes next to a bottle of wine with a Picasso-inspired skewed neck.

Johnny heard footsteps rumbling around in the apartment above the restaurant. His nephew Nino was visiting from Italy. He would prepare him breakfast.

Johnny walked into the kitchen and turned on the burner. The gas flame jumped to attention. A fleeting thought came to him. Jewish lighting was always an option. A grease fire was not unheard of. But a fleeting thought was all it was. Still, he made a mental note to check his fire insurance.

He cracked eggs deftly into a cast-iron pan, scrambling the yolk into an omelet. He added mozzarella, along with a variety of condiments. Simultaneously, stale Italian bread was put in a toaster. As the eggs simmered, he prepared the coffee. The cappuccino machine whistled as the frothy steamed milk flowed into the cups. Johnny Paradise was a multi-tasker. He'd grown up in this restaurant, learning all he knew from his father. His nephew would be coming down any moment. He had arrived from Italy and would be staying a few weeks, trying to get a business venture off the ground.

"*Buon giorno, Zio.*" Johnny embraced his nephew and kissed his cheek. It was like looking in a mirror that brought him back thirty years. His nephew had deep-set black-cat eyes, an olive complexion, and an inviting smile—a mirror image of the portrait. The bloodline was without doubt.

"Did you sleep well?" Johnny asked.

"Difficult to sleep with all the sirens."

"Ah," affirmed his uncle. The competing symphony of police cars and ambulance sirens were white noise for him but took some getting used to by a visitor. Emergency vehicles were kept busy in this neighborhood. Nino followed his uncle into the dining room. "I've prepared breakfast."

"So, what is in store for today? How can I help?" Nino asked.

Johnny slid the omelet into dishes, and brought the toast and butter to the table as well as the coffee. "Well, today is Friday. There are not too many reservations. You don't have to stay around if you have something more important to tend to. Go into Manhattan. Otherwise you're welcome to stay. Nothing exciting in store." As an afterthought, he added, "The Romeo Club will come in for lunch."

Nino repeated, "The Romeo Club?"

"Ah, yes. They're regulars. Best I should give you a heads-up. They are the most juvenile, unruly group you will ever meet. Two are Italian, and the third thinks he is or wishes he were. You will hear the stupidest jokes that will get the loudest laughs directly commensurate with the amount of alcohol consumed, and consume they will. They will complain about everything. The bread will be stale, the pasta over-cooked, the chicken under-cooked. The calamari will be chewy. The service will be too slow, or they will complain about being rushed. The red wine will definitely be corked. They will get into a deep philosophical discussion on whether it's permissible to put grated cheese on linguine with white clam sauce. There are two schools of thought on the subject. They will tell you how the *pasta fagioli* should be made, like their mother did. They will make the sign of the cross at the very mention of their mothers. The fresh-roasted peppers, they will claim, are pimentos from a can, and the hot peppers, oh, the hot peppers will not be hot enough. For this though, I have a remedy today."

Nino was enjoying the omelet, using bread to push it onto his fork. He shook his head and shrugged. "Zio, I need to ask. Why do you put up with this?"

Johnny Paradise recoiled. "Nino," he said, confused by the question, "they're my friends."

Johnny Paradise had named them The Romeo Club; Restless Old Men Eating Out. They were personal friends going back thirty years, as close to him as they were to each other. They shared two afflictions that were common among well-heeled, middle-aged men—two of the most potentially destructive forces known to man: boredom and free time. "There are many ways men choose to remedy this affliction," Johnny explained. "Some men leave their wives; others just add various women while keeping their wives. Considering all manner of temptation, decadence, and debauchery there is to choose from, a few hours of food, wine, and laughs seems harmless—liver, heart, and kidneys notwithstanding," Johnny added.

For these charter members of the Romeo Club, after years of hard work, life was good. It was their version of a three-martini lunch, on steroids. They were all in their mid-sixties, and the camaraderie was life sustaining. Although each was successful in their respective field, life had a monotony, a dreary sameness that was masked by their friendship and time together. Now, in the throes of winter, each, in his own way, sought to answer Peggy Lee's musical question, "Is that all there is?" As snow covered the greens at the local golf course—and their temples—they gravitated for a quick bite that would turn into a laugh fest. The very definition of reality television, complete with reruns.

Ever in sync, three cars pulled into the parking lot. Frankie Grace, a local funeral director, bundled his overcoat against the winter wind and walked into the restaurant. He was followed by Dr. Claudio Odelli, a general practitioner. For these childlike minds, *Claudio* plus *doctor* plus *Odelli* added up to "Cardio." So, *Cardio* it was.

Frankie handed his coat to Marco, the waiter, along with a bouquet of flowers wrapped in paper. Marco would trim the stems and place a flower in the vase on each table.

"*Gracias*," Marco said.

"Don't thank me. Thank Mrs. DeLuca."

Johnny stepped up to introduce his friends. "Nino, meet Mr. Grace. He's my friend and undertaker," he said, smiling. In keeping with an old-world Italian tradition, Nino scratched his crotch after shaking hands with Frankie. It was a superstition meant to ward off *malocchio*, the evil eye. The meaning was, basically, "Undertaker, bad." Johnny had long ago given up on the practice. Being in Frankie's company so often made it problematic.

Doctor Cardio was right behind. "And this is Dr. Claudio Odelli." There was a note of pride in his voice as he emphasized "doctor."

The doctor was a tall, lanky man with rimless eyeglasses. He handed Marco his coat and fedora. "Thank you, my good fellow," he said, ever the gentleman. His suit was accented by a pocket square, vest, and red bowtie that might have been fashionable a generation or two earlier. Lagging behind was Timmy Collins, wearing a sport jacket and oversized yellow knit scarf wrapped twice around his neck. He was involved in a discussion on his cell phone as he walked around the parking lot, gesticulating wildly.

Timmy walked through the door with the flair of Carson stepping on stage from behind the curtain on *The Tonight Show*. He was crooning "Fly Me to the Moon." A cigar dangled from his fingertips. Dean Martin had nothing on Tim Collins.

"Hey, Johnny," hardly noticing the young man, "when you gonna take down the Christmas lights? It's friggin' February." Indeed, the strings of blue, red, and green bulbs encircled every hedge surrounding the building and seemed seamlessly connected to the string that encircled the bar and overhead rack, from which stemware dangled.

Calmly, Johnny responded, "My customers like them. They add to the ambiance."

"Ambiance?" Frankie repeated. "Must be the French word for dust." He ran a finger along the molding.

"He has dust brought in once a week, for authenticity," Timmy quipped.

"You are funny men," Johnny said as everyone laughed.

Dr. Odelli finally asked, "Who's this young man?"

Johnny's chest expanded. "This is my nephew Nino, from Italy. He's staying with me for a few weeks to work on a business venture."

"What kind of business? You need investors?" Timmy asked. Tim Collins was a real estate developer and broker. Always looking for new opportunities.

The young man greeted them politely. "I am Nino Paradiso. It is a pleasure. I have heard much about all of you. I am director of Eremo di San Calogero, a clinic in Italy specializing in healing and rejuvenation."

"Rejuvenate this," Timmy said pointing to his zipper.

"He said 'rejuvenate,' not 'resurrect,'" Frankie said.

"You still got it," Johnny said.

"You are a funny man," Timmy agreed. "I need a drink. Get rid of those Christmas lights. Marco, your best bottle of cheap wine!" Everyone laughed, as if they had never heard it before.

The three men moved to the corner table set for six. Invariably, they would invite someone to join them.

Marco the waiter brought the large chalkboard with the day's specials. "The only thing that changed from last week is the price," Frankie said.

"Food is a commodity," Johnny reminded him.

Frankie Grace was tasked with the appetizer order, fried calamari, eggplant rollatini, arancini and baked clams, etc. "This should tide us over until the main course," he explained. The food kept coming. Appetizers were followed by a platter of pasta, rigatoni, family style. Try as he might to get it right, Marco would make some mistake placing the admittedly complicated order. That would lead to good-natured threats, which he, too, took in stride.

"When we build the wall, Marco, I'm gonna drive you to the border and personally see to it you get back to Mexico," Tim threatened. Marco had a good nature, and his ability to run with the bulls gave him staying power. He was part of the extended Paradise family. He could take it; he could give it back.

"But, I am Ecuadorian, not Mexican," he explained.

"Same difference," Timmy responded.

"Try the baked clams," Cardio suggested as he ran a piece of bread through the dish, soaking up the remnant juices. "Delicious," he said.

"Nothing like Italian food," Frankie agreed. "You never hear anyone say, 'Let's go out for Irish tonight.' That brought a smirk from Collins, as he projected his middle finger.

"Who are you kidding? You know you always wanted to be Italian," Cardio reminded him.

"Maybe I am. I'm gonna get my genes tested."

"You do that," Frankie said, "and get your shirts tested, too."

"You're a funny man," Collins said as they giggled like kindergartners.

Cardio observed, "You may have some Italian blood. You got the biggest nose I've ever seen on an Irishman."

"When he was born, the doctor thought it was a third arm," Frankie said.

"What luck," Collins complained. "My undertaker is a comedian."

"A comedian is what I am. It's just not what I do," Frankie said.

Marco brought more wine to the table. The jokes, indeed, got funnier in direct proportion to the wine consumption, as Johnny Paradise had predicted.

A Con Edison worker walked into the restaurant and placed his blue hard hat on the bar. "Hey," Timmy yelled, "what's blue and white and sleeps nine people?"

"A Con Edison Truck," the man said, without hesitation.

"Oh, you've heard it before?" Tim said.

The man nodded. "Last week, when I came in for lunch. You told me the same joke."

Marco handed the man a box with hero sandwiches. "No charge," Johnny said. "Lunch is on them today." The man tipped his hat.

In the middle of the madness, Timmy's cell phone started to sing. He was conducting last-minute business, placing bets, reviewing odds as the Super Bowl loomed. He walked away from the table so he could hear and be heard.

Paradise took all the complaints in stride. As it turned out, the wine was corked and warm, the pasta too mushy, the bread stale, the peppers weren't hot enough.

"I just buy them," he explained. "Sometimes they're hot, sometimes they're not. There's no writing on them." These were his friends, and ball-breaking came with the territory. But he had a way of getting even.

Paradise whispered to Marco, "Get the peppers I bought yesterday; serve them." Marco's eyes opened wide. He leaned into Johnny, thinking he'd misheard the request. "Just do it," Paradise said.

In a moment, the reluctant waiter came out of the kitchen with a dish of peppers. The aroma by itself spelled danger. The heat manifested into a steamy haze hanging over the dish. He walked slowly, questioning Paradise's decision with each step, hoping he'd change his mind.

"Try these, guys," Johnny said. "I think they're hot." The peppers were small, crimson red, unassuming. Looking closely might have revealed the word "danger" on their stem. Paradise knew they measured at the highest end of the Scoville scale. He had done his homework. Tim, Frankie, and Cardio popped them into their mouths. In a moment, all conversation ceased. It took only seconds before the coughing and gagging started. Cardio poured water down his throat. "No," Frankie yelled, his voice straining. "That makes it worse." Collins emptied salt on bread. "Milk, milk," Frankie called to Marco. Marco did not rush into the kitchen.

"*No comprende*," he said, mimicking his own stereotype. Paradise leaned against the bar, watching tears flow down the faces of his friends. "Priceless," he said to his nephew.

"Are you trying to kill us?" Cardio asked. His voice was scratchy.

"Oh," Johnny asked, "did you get a hot one?" Their faces were beet red, sweat prickled their foreheads, tears ran down their cheeks. "Good, huh?" he said, enjoying every moment of their anguish. He slapped Nino on the back.

Copious pitchers of water could not extinguish the flame; indeed, it made it worse. Loaves of bread—even wiping napkins across their tongues did not help.

"You *are* trying to kill us?" Timmy cried. His voice caught up in his windpipe.

They coughed and gagged as pressure built in their faces like a boiler ready to blow. It took a good half hour for the burn to subside, and each knew they would feel the effects again before the day was over.

Following the meal, Marco brought ricotta cheesecake, espresso, anisette, cognac, and Port. Only ice figurines at a wedding's Venetian hour were missing. There were hugs all around as Cardio figured out the check. Each man shared the check, adding a generous tip. Frankie and Cardio threw a credit card in, and Tim paid his share in cash. As was his practice, Tim slipped Marco an extra twenty. He considered it a ball-breaking surcharge. "*A domani!*" Frankie said.

"Who do you guys like Sunday?" Timmy asked as they staggered out. "Anyone want to come over to watch the game?"

"I'm gonna relax at home," Cardio said. "I know nothing about sports."

"You're a nerd," Timmy said. "You've never known anything about sports for as long as I've known you."

"Anyway, you look tired," Frankie observed. "You should go home. Get some rest."

"I am a little tired," Cardio admitted. "But I have one more appointment."

"I may still score on tickets to the game. I'll know later today, tomorrow at the latest," Timmy said.

"You got a lot riding on it?" Cardio asked.

"Let's just say lunch is on me Monday," he answered.

"What about you, Frankie? Any plans?" Cardio asked.

"Working tomorrow. I accepted a call from the public administrator to bury an unclaimed body. I have to go to Veterans Cemetery, way out on Long Island. Should be finished by noon, one the latest. I'll call to see if you guys are around."

As the Romeo Club dispersed from Paradise's Italian Restaurant, Nino turned to his uncle. "Incredible. You were right, *zio*. Inside every man there is a little boy, *un piccolo bambino*. I thought they would never leave."

Johnny looked at the clock. "Don't worry. They'll be back for cocktails at five. Happy hour."

⁕

Chapter III

After lunch, *Doctor Claudio Odelli was sitting* at his desk, staring at the photos of his wife. There were no patients scheduled. The last of a breed, Doctor Odelli was beloved by his patients, who grew old with him over a practice of forty years. He was the "Marcus Welby" of his generation, the last of the family doctors who spent time with patients, spoke with them, and more importantly, listened. His patients ranged from the wealthy to the poorest of the poor. Now at age sixty-five, he found he couldn't deal with the Obamacare-style practice that kept him busy doing paperwork and dealing with insurance companies. He preferred caring for people, not paper. Rather than a well-deserved retirement, he became a concierge physician. He kept a select number of patients, who paid a yearly fee. In return, they got his undivided attention. He thought he'd be able to stay active for a few more years, anyway. His next appointment would make it all moot.

The meeting was with his own physician, with whom he had just undergone a battery of tests at New York's Sloan Kettering. Odelli was a practical man. Having a friend and physician stop by his office was not a good sign. He heard a tentative knock on his door. The look on his colleague's face was revealing—undertaker grim. There was a firm handshake that lingered and avoiding eyes. Together they stared at the illuminated X-ray of a human skull on the wall.

His colleague spoke. "It's rare, as you know. Only 5,000 people in the United States."

Cardio remembered hearing the diagnosis, and not hearing it at all. The doctor droned on, but the sound evaporated. He was overwhelmed. The doctor's lips were moving, but Cardio was lost, his mind drifting. Cardio felt a knot in his stomach, a tremor in his legs. His brain reprised the words: "incurable," "fatal." They ruminated in his mind. His associate murmured on about possible treatments that showed some promise. An experimental drug called Riluzole was working its way through testing for FDA approval. Claudio knew better. Even someone with a degree from St. George's University School of Medicine in Grenada understood the diagnosis and the future that awaited him. His colleague's words disappeared into the air. He was surprised by his own lack of response—perhaps because he knew what the diagnosis would be. Hearing it officially was perfunctory.

"Claudio, Claudio . . ." The doctor attempted to bring Odelli back into the moment. "What's your plan? What are you going to do? We will have to start right away. An exercise program . . ."

Odelli rose from his seat and adjusted his bowtie, straightened his vest. In the steadiest of voices, revealing no quaver, or concern, he answered, "Yes, yes—I understand. Thank you, my friend," he said as he walked him to the door.

✳

Chapter IV

The Grace Funeral Home was a majestic, three-story Colonial surrounded by a manicured lawn and pristine landscaping. It was a one-man operation that Frankie had owned for forty years. He'd found the small town accidentally. He helped an elderly funeral director from Inlet Cove by delivering a body from New York's Bellevue. The owner was a kindly gentleman who invited Frankie to lunch at a local pizzeria. Frankie, a product of Manhattan's Little Italy, was a pizza snob. Surely, this hick town couldn't compete, but, out of respect, he accommodated the man. There, over a slice of pizza, began a conversation that resulted in Frankie's buying the man's establishment and moving from Manhattan to Inlet Cove. The move was necessary. The small storefront funeral home on Manhattan's lower east side wasn't generating business after three generations. The clientele dried up—in prison or previously buried. The Italian neighborhood was beginning to change, so he seized the opportunity. It proved to be a lucky slice of pizza. In the near-forty years that followed, Frankie became a well-respected member of the Inlet Cove community. And, surprisingly, the pizza wasn't bad.

Inlet Cove was a quaint hamlet boasting a scenic harbor on Long Island Sound. Across the harbor, the Throgs Neck and Whitestone bridges were visible to the south. It was a small community, where everyone knew everyone. Behind the home, there was a large parking area. The main floor had two reposing rooms. An office, embalming room, and casket-selection room occupied the basement. The top floor served as living quarters, with the parlor converted to a spacious office, complete with a fully stocked bar and espresso machine. Frankie's wife wintered in Florida and had begun to summer there as well. He'd go back and forth as his schedule would allow. Truth be told, he wasn't ready for the Florida lifestyle. *God's waiting room*, he called it. There was more to life than golf every day; plus, he didn't have the network of friends there.

Photographs were hanging on the mahogany-paneled walls. Photographs of his old neighborhood on Mulberry Street in Manhattan. He grew up in Little Italy, twenty-five miles from where he now sat, but it was a three-hour drive on any given day. These photographs were the only link to those days. He had not been back for fifteen years, since his mother had died. There was no reason. He always looked at the photographs and remembered his father's admonishment: "Go where you have to go in life, but never forget where you came from." That's what these photographs did for him. They kept him grounded. Overhead photos of The Feast of San Gennaro, the crowds, the concessions. He could see the smoke from the sausage cooking on grills, and he could even taste it. There were pictures of his mother and father. His father would have been proud of Frankie's success in the funeral profession.

Dealing with the dead wasn't Frankie's first career choice, much to his father's consternation. Frankie was naturally funny and thought he could parlay his role as class clown into a career as a stand-up comedian. The prospects for a comedian in the funeral family were grim. The very thought gave his father chest pains. In the end, though, he accepted the torch and hoped his father knew that the third generation in funeral business was secure. He had carried on the family business.

Yet, he could not help but also wonder what would have become of him if he had pursued the other path. Stand-up comedy was certainly a long shot—no guarantees, but he showed some promise early on, played some big rooms, opened for bona fide headliners at mob-owned lounges, but in the end, it seemed a higher power had other plans for him.

Frankie got an early start Saturday morning. The public administrator of Westchester County, Albert Gregoria, had called Frankie, explaining, "If you don't help, I'll have to send him to Potter's Field." The thought of anyone being buried in an unmarked grave on Hart Island, dug by prisoners from Rikers, made the hair on Frankie's neck stand at attention.

"What do you say, Frankie?" Gregoria asked. "*Greatest Generation* and all that," he coaxed. But he knew the answer. Frankie Grace always said "Yes," accepting the call pro-bono. It was his way of giving back.

A jaded attendant at the medical examiner's office yawned and looked over the paperwork giving Frankie Grace authority to remove the unclaimed body of Robert Taffy.

"Jesus," the man said, "I ain't even had my coffee. It's six o'clock, man!"

"Sorry," Frankie explained, "the cemetery is hours away and I have lots of work to do to get him ready." The attendant led him down antiseptic tiled hallway with refrigerated morgue boxes on both sides. He opened one and pulled out a tray with the deceased wrapped in white plastic. "He's ripe," the attendant said. "Being dead for more than three weeks will do that to you."

Frankie maneuvered the body onto his stretcher and into his van. The strong stench of death mixing with Clorox and other antiseptics used to clean the morgue would stay with him for hours. Embalming the vet was not necessary, but Frankie thought he owed him as much. He wanted to do right by the colonel. Frankie was old school. It was ingrained in him that, as an undertaker, he had to especially care for those who had no one to care for them.

The colonel's arteries had collapsed, and it took a six-point injection through axillaries, femoral, and carotid arteries to get fluid into him. He posed his features, gently closing the eyes and mouth. He shaved him and trimmed his mustache. After a few hours in the prep room, Colonel Taffy looked good as new, considering he had been dead for weeks. The odor had subsided. Frankie found a casket with a small scratch. It was an upgrade from the doeskin-covered plywood that the county allowed. He buffed it out. Brand new. He dressed the vet in a new suit, placed him in the formerly damaged casket, and draped it with an American Flag. He had ordered a small red, white, and blue bouquet and placed it near the casket.

Back in his office, Frankie affixed his signature to the burial permit. Near his desk there were twelve screens that recorded and flashed real-time images of the funeral home inside and out. There were similar monitors throughout the funeral home in strategic locations. He saw a car come across the monitors. It was Reverend White.

The reverend made his way up to Frankie's office. Frankie prepared two cups of espresso. He added Sambuca and handed one to the reverend as he appeared in the doorway. "Have a seat, reverend. I'm waiting for the hearse."

"What's the story, Frankie? Where is everyone? I saw the casket, but there's no one in the chapel with him." The reverend made himself comfortable.

"That's just it, reverend. He had no family. He died alone. I volunteered to take care of his burial. I thought it would be nice to say a prayer for him before we left."

"Poor soul," he said. The reverend walked to the cabinet and poured more Sambuca into his cup. "You're a good man, Frankie."

"Well, he must have been quite a guy," Frankie said. "I read his discharge papers. Turns out he marched with Patton's army and received two Purple Hearts. When neighbors noticed an odor coming from his apartment, they called the police. He's been languishing in the morgue waiting for a family member to step up. None did. So, I volunteered my services."

"A prayer couldn't hurt," the reverend said. He slugged the Sambuca down and then another; then he topped his cup with another taste. "I always love coming here," he said.

Frankie acknowledged with a nod and a smile. "I wonder why?" Frankie saw the hearse on the security camera pull into the parking lot. "Time to go," Frankie said.

The two men stood before the flag-draped casket. Frankie bowed his head as Reverend White gave a slurred version of the Lord's Prayer and final benediction. After the blessing, Frankie rolled the flag-draped casket into the hearse.

"Reverend, do you have time for lunch? I'll be back by one?"

"No, Frankie. The last time you took me to lunch, I got back to the rectory after five o'clock, and the pastor was not too happy."

"That's only because he wasn't invited."

They both laughed. The hearse pulled away as Frankie waved. "If you change your mind, meet me in Paradise." He looked at his watch and estimated two hours out to Calverton, Long Island, two hours back. With any luck and no traffic, he'd be back in time for lunch.

❄   ❄   ❄

At the Calverton National Veterans Cemetery, all aspects of the burial were handled with military precision. On cue, an Army corpsman in the distance sounded "Taps." It echoed hauntingly through the snow-capped pine trees, the notes clinging to a gust of snow propelled by a winter wind. Frankie still got goosebumps at the somberness of the ceremony. He considered that a good sign. He wasn't hardened or inured yet. Afterward, two cadets marched to positions at the head and foot of the casket. With reverence, they lifted the flag, stepped to the side, and began folding it, thirteen times, representing the original colonies. One to the other, they saluted and accepted the folded flag; then they pivoted over to Frankie. He was the only one there. The flag was presented to him on behalf of a grateful nation. He accepted the flag. The two-hour ride from Westchester to Calverton, Long Island was well worth it.

Back home, Frankie took the flag and brought it to the local VFW. A group of elderly men were sitting in a community room, some playing board games, others playing cards, others staring pointlessly into space. He saw his future. Frankie handed the flag to the bartender, suggesting it be flown on the flagpole in front of the building, in memory of the colonel. The man saluted Frankie and poured him a shot of Dewar's. "To the colonel," Frankie said.

※

Chapter V

Frankie Grace wasn't the only one headed to a cemetery on Saturday morning. Dr. Odelli drove into St. Mary's Cemetery and stopped alongside the road. Breaking unwritten rules of solemnity, he turned up the volume on the car radio. She loved music, dancing, singing. Why not? It was his way of letting her know he was there. Each song brought its own memory. He took a bouquet of flowers from the front seat and proceeded down a path lined with dates and dashes. The walk was increasingly problematic as the pitted ground beneath his feet became more of a challenge to traverse. He paused, placing the flower in front of a stone that read:

KATHLEEN ODELLI

1953–2000

Beloved wife

With a handkerchief, he wiped the stone clean and then bowed his head. He made a mental note to ensure there was room for the next inscription.

※

Chapter VI

On that fateful Sunday evening, Timmy Collins slumped zombie-like in a recliner chair, staring at the television. He was wearing a velour jogging suit that he never used for jogging and white sweat socks. An unlit cigar had fallen from his lip and lay on his chest. An empty bottle of Jack Daniels was on a table at his side. He was stunned and dumbfounded. The improbable had happened. Of course, it did. Foles had led the Eagles to an upset win. Oblivious to his wife, Tracy, calling from the kitchen, oblivious to Frank Sinatra singing "Fly Me to the Moon," causing his phone to dance on the end table, he sat hypnotized, comatose, bewitched, bothered, and bewildered.

❊

Chapter VII

On Monday, Frankie Grace pulled up to Johnny Paradise's. He was talking to his wife on his cell phone. The washing machine was acting up. He didn't know what he could do, inasmuch as he was 1300 miles away and not mechanically inclined. "Call a repairman," he suggested. He understood her dire emergency; having a washing machine on the fritz was a life-altering event to his wife. "In the meantime, use the other washing machine," he suggested. In the laundry room at his Florida home, there were two washers and two dryers—just in case. "No, no," he said into the phone. "Odds are the other one won't go down, too. That's why we did it." His wife would be the first to admit she had OCD—so much so that she reordered the letters to CDO to keep them in alphabetical order. With the washing-machine crisis expertly handled, he said goodbye. She'd be calling again to complain that the repairman's schedule did not match hers. Even if he were there, he'd be no help. Frankie had an adversarial relationship with tools, toolboxes, skill saws, or pliers. He didn't know one end of a screwdriver from the other. He had no workshop, no work bench, and generally needed three estimates to change a lightbulb.

Cardio parked alongside Frankie. The two men chatted for a moment as Tim pulled into the lot. He jumped out of the car.

"Hey, guys. How was the weekend?" His phone sang from within his pocket. "Go in. I'll be right there." He took out a cigar, and this time, he lit it.

"I thought you gave those up." Cardio said. "They will kill you."

"Why would I take advice from a guy with a medical degree from the University of Guam? Are you even a doctor?" It was vintage Timmy.

"It was Grenada, and I've kept you alive," Cardio retorted.

"For now," he said. He waved them in. "Don't worry. If you live long enough, you gotta die from something," he answered. "Go in. I'll catch up."

"Does he seem more hyper than usual?" Cardio asked.

"Hard to tell with him," Frankie said.

"Welcome to Paradise," Johnny greeted them. Nino was behind the bar. Paradise gestured with his eyebrows and slight tilt of his head toward an occupied table, in the corner, near a rear exit. "You see who's there?"

Frankie nodded, as did Cardio, just as Timmy entered. They all recognized the gentleman sitting at the table near the rear-exit door. It was Sam Napoli. He was tanned, with slicked-back hair and polished nails that reflected the light. He was wearing a beautiful suit—a Brioni, Frankie guessed—and a white voile shirt with a long collar that hid the knot on his tie. The gentleman with him was wearing pedestrian clothing, a plaid shirt, jeans, and work boots. At a table on each side of Napoli, out of earshot, were two formidable-looking bodyguards.

Sam Napoli was godfather emeritus, captain of a mafia family that bore his name. The aging don's deep, abiding friendship with Johnny Paradise had been cemented years earlier, when Paradise senior, whose portrait adorned the bar, took a rap, kept his mouth shut, served his time, and was released. His freedom was short-lived. For his loyalty, he was rewarded with a bullet in his head. His body turned up in a trunk at Kennedy Airport. Rumor had it that don Napoli even shed a tear at the funeral home and vowed to take vengeance on the murderers of his dear friend and associate. The search for the killer was still in progress. These things take time. Still, that friendship ensured that Johnny Paradise, Jr. was in the protectorate of don Napoli. No one could put the arm on Johnny Paradise. Paradise used his own purveyors and vendors, chose his own sanitation company and linen company, and paid no royalty—not even for the antique jukebox which, like the don, was a reminder of older days.

"We best go say hello," Frankie said.

"Don't all go at once," Paradise advised. "You don't want to spook the gorillas." The two bodyguards, complete with dark glasses, pitted complexions, and big knuckles, stared at them as Johnny spoke. Their heads turned like oscillating fans as they meticulously surveyed the dining room as their boss held a conversation with the man at his table. "Believe me," Paradise added, "those guys can scratch their knees without bending."

Frankie walked over first. Napoli knew of Frankie's *family ties* going back to when he was younger, on New York's lower east side. This was, after all, a close-knit community. As Frankie approached, the apes stirred. Napoli gestured them down and stood up to greet Frankie, introducing him jokingly to his associate at the table as his undertaker. He laughed. "How many people can say they know their undertaker?"

Frankie kissed the don and accepted his gentle pat on the cheek. "You gotta be more careful who you hang out with," he said, laughing and pointing. Cardio and Timmy approached and went through the same kissing ritual. "You being good?" He directed the question to Timmy. "I don't hear good things. Word is you had a tough night. Maybe it's best you stay close to a doctor and undertaker. You never know when you may need them."

Everyone laughed. Timmy's laugh got caught in his throat. After a few more pleasantries and non-introduction of the don's guest, everyone retreated to their corners.

Back at their table, the conversation became a bit tempered as the men watched a special news alert on the television behind the bar. World-famous chef Anthony Bourdain had committed suicide.

"I don't understand these guys, Bourdain, Robin Williams," Timmy said. "They got it all. Fame, wealth, broads, more broads, everything to live for—and they off themselves. They don't know how to live."

"It's not the 'how,'" Cardio suggested, "It's the 'why.' They lost the 'why' to live."

"Too deep for me, Doc," Tim said.

"It's certainly ironic," Frankie said. "The bravest—and, at the same time, most selfish—thing you can do. Believe me, it takes a pair to kill yourself."

"Yeah," Cardio chimed in. "Life sucks sometimes. It turns on a dime. You're going along fine. You think you got it all figured out, got the world by the balls; then they find a bump on your ass or a spot on your lung. God only knows what they were facing, or thought they were facing. You gotta walk in their shoes." The words settled in for a moment as they stared at the images flashing on the television.

It was Timmy who broke the spell. "Marco, your best bottle of cheap wine!" But it was only an expression. For the members of the Romeo Club, life was too short to drink cheap wine.

A few customers strolled in. Two young women went to a table farthest from them. "How surprising," Marco observed.

"Shouldn't you be bringing bread to their table or something?" Tim suggested.

"*Si, señor*," Marco said, again mimicking the caricature. Another couple made their way to a table in the center of the room.

During lunch, Timmy's phone kept singing. At one point, he put it on vibrate. He was fidgety and distracted. "I'm going for a smoke," he said as he left the table.

"Since when did you start up again? Those things will kill you," Cardio warned.

"I told you, if you live long enough, you'll die of something."

"Amen," Frankie answered.

"Besides," Timmy added as he left the table, "you're not even a real doctor."

The remark was met by Cardio's middle finger. Having gone to medical school in Grenada was a constant source of ball-breaking for him. But Claudio's youthful lack of motivation produced less-than-stellar undergraduate grades, and, for Claudio, with his few financial resources, Grenada was more inviting.

Frankie and Cardio began to eat. Frankie poured wine and inquired as to Cardio's day. "You busy?"

"A patient or two," he answered. "Even that's getting to be too much. I think it's time to throw in the towel."

"Retire? You mean *retire*?"

"Maybe," the doctor said.

"Geeze," Frankie answered. "I never heard you talk like that. You feeling okay?"

It was a generic question, but as Frankie stared at his friend, he saw something odd, a twitch in his neck, a drooping jaw, but it had no time to register.

In the foreground, through the restaurant's tinted window, beneath the intermittent glow of the neon sign, Timmy's torso moved back and forth like a rubber duck in a carnival trailer. A cigar was dangling from his lips. The phone was cemented to his ear.

Frankie thought nothing of the screeching sound of tires coming to an abrupt halt. Then, for a microsecond, the time between two breaths, the Earth stopped. Then the crackling sound of fireworks engulfed them. The next few seconds played out as if in slow motion. Timmy disappeared from the window frame as the glass exploded. Projectiles ricocheted throughout the dining room. Customers fell to the floor. Bottles and glasses shattered as glass fragments jingled off the shelves. Marco leaped into the kitchen. Frankie and Cardio dove behind the table and Johnny Paradise behind the bar, falling on his nephew to cover him. Then silence, dead silence, until the sound of screeching tires became faint as the last piece of shattered glass landed as if to punctuate the moment. As each patron began to realize what had just happened, shock turned to panic and then into screams.

Johnny Paradise peeked his head out from the bar. He looked to the back table. Sam Napoli and company were gone, leaving the exit door swinging. More tires screeched from the parking lot.

"Is everyone okay?" Paradise shouted. He heard full-throated screams from the women who had fallen to the floor for cover. Cardio ran over to assess their injuries. They were shaking, but he saw no outward signs of wounds. Cardio looked back to Frankie, who was quickly approaching. He froze in place as he looked at Cardio. They had the same thought, and, together, they both spoke the word, "Timmy!"

Johnny and Nino bolted from behind the bar, and the men ran outside. The smell of gunpowder filled the air. "Jesus!" Johnny yelled, pointing to the body slumped in the hydrangea bushes.

"Timmy, Timmy!" The men were too paralyzed to move. Sirens droned in the distance. Stunned, they walked fearfully toward the body, part of them not wanting to know. Not until there was movement did they breathe.

Timmy began to extricate himself from the bush. A sprig of holly and a string of Christmas lights were encircling his head like a crown of thorns. His hairpiece was askew, dangling off his brow. His friends moved more quickly now to help him. There was blood on his face from the thorns but no other signs of injury. Cardio took his pulse. "Calm down, Timmy. Your heart is racing. Calm down." Tim's hands were shaking.

Three police cars pulled into the parking lot. "We need an ambulance!" Cardio ordered. An officer called for one, as the others ran into the restaurant. Quickly, they assessed there was no active shooter on the premises. They had first-aid kits.

"EMS is on the way," an officer called out.

Inside the dining room, patrons had calmed down; officers were sitting with them, taking notes.

Nino brought a chair outside, and they helped Timmy into it. "Timmy, we need to get you to a hospital. Your heart is racing," Cardio said.

"No, I'm fine."

"Bull—you're not fine," the doctor insisted.

"Sir, can you tell me what happened here?" It was a police sergeant.

Timmy was stammering. "A black van pulled up, the door opened, and boom, boom, boom."

"How many people?" the sergeant asked.

"I don't know. One, two. One, I think. He had a canon and just kept firing."

"You get a look at him?"

"Hood, ski mask," Tim said.

The sergeant turned to Johnny. "What did you see, Johnny?"

"Just like he said. We were inside. One minute it was quiet, and, then, it was World War III."

"How many people were in the dining room?" the sergeant asked.

"Just a small group. These guys, my nephew. Timmy went out for a smoke. A deuce at table four, another at table six and Sammy . . ." As he said the name, his voice trailed off as the implications became clear.

"Sammy . . . ," the sergeant prodded.

"Sammy Napoli was here with a guest," Johnny admitted. The men all exchanged glances. "A hit? An attempted hit?" Johnny wondered out loud.

"Is he still in there?" the sergeant asked

"Actually, no. Uh, he had a take-out order," Johnny offered.

"Or, somebody did," Frankie added.

Two more ambulances pulled into the parking lot. The diners inside refused any medical attention. They just wanted to get out of there as soon as possible. Johnny hated to lose what few customers he had. "I'm so sorry, folks," he said. "The appetizers are on me, and here is a gift certificate . . ." They left the red-velvet drapes swaying before he could finish. He understood. It was lame.

Timmy resisted but finally relented, and Cardio jumped in the back of the ambulance with him. "I'll catch up later," Frankie said. "Are you sure you're all right?" he asked his friend. They heard Frank Sinatra singing "Fly Me to the Moon" over in the bushes.

"Would you grab my phone, Frankie?"

Frankie searched the hedges. He found the phone and walked it over to the ambulance. He looked down and noticed the caller: *Sergi*. He thought nothing of it.

Inside the restaurant, Nino had poured himself a drink and one for his uncle. "Are you okay, *nepote*?" his uncle asked.

His nephew looked at him. "Does this happen often?"

Johnny smiled and hugged him. "Welcome to America."

They laughed an uneasy laugh as they drank and stared at the portrait of their patriarch behind the bar. A bullet had pierced the velvet canvas, leaving a hole directly in the forehead. They exchanged glances. The not-so-subtle irony did not escape them; art had, indeed, imitated life.

✳　✳　✳

A crew from News 12 pulled into the parking lot, and a reporter and cameramen set up for a live feed.

"Christ!" Nino said. "That didn't take long."

"News travels," Johnny explained. "Bad news travels faster." He went outside, knowing he'd have to answer some questions and be smart about it. Until now, the biggest news in this town was the opening of a petting zoo at the local park.

"What can you tell us, Mr. Paradise?" A female reporter shoved a microphone in his face.

"Not much," he said. "Probably a random act of violence."

"Was anyone hurt?"

"No, just shaken up, as you might imagine. One man did go to the hospital, but he did not suffer any wounds. It was precautionary."

"Mr. Paradise, is it true that Sam Napoli was in the restaurant? Was this a mob hit? Was this a rubout attempt?"

Johnny caught his breath. "No, no. Mr. Napoli was not in the restaurant at the time. He'd left long before the incident. This was just a random act of violence. For all I know, they had the wrong address, or it was just some kids shooting up the neighborhood. They probably got us mixed up with the bodega down the street. There's a shooting there every day."

"Thank you, Mr. Paradise." The reporter turned and stared into the camera. "Once again, we are live from Johnny Paradise's Italian Restaurant, where police suspect there was an attempted rubout of mafia boss Sam Napoli."

Johnny shook his head. "Did she hear anything I just said?" he asked Nino.

※

Chapter VIII

Timmy Collins was not an ideal patient. He'd fought every attempt to have him admitted into the hospital. He was hooked up to a monitor that measured his heart rate. Red and green lights matched intermittent beeping. Because of his history of high blood pressure and stents, his friend and doctor was concerned. "Just for the night, for observation," Cardio pleaded as he adjusted the intravenous tube.

"No way, no way." Tim was adamant.

Cardio gave him an injection to calm him. "I called Tracy. She's on her way."

"What did you tell her? Hope you didn't scare her. She's not good with things like this. We're already going through a rough patch. She's probably worried sick. Did you tell her I'm all right? Poor thing. She must be a nervous wreck. When did you call?"

"I called from the ambulance. What could that be, an hour ago, hour and a half, at the most?"

The answer hung out there for a moment.

"Traffic," Timmy suggested, looking for affirmation.

Cardio nodded, "I guess."

"Get me signed out of here," Timmy said. "I'll go home with her."

"I'm your doctor," he said. "I think you should stay overnight."

He left the room as Tim yelled, "I'm not taking advice from a doctor from Granada."

"It's Grenada," Cardio yelled back. As he turned, he came face to face with a buttoned-down, pasty-faced man with a thin mustache.

"Can I have a word with you, doctor? I'm agent Reno Amore." He flashed his credentials. Cardio saw the letters "FBI" clearly.

"Not right now," Cardio said as he whisked past him.

In the midst of the confusion in the emergency room, Frankie was brought into an office. The investigation had been kicked up to a new level. The local police were not the lead agency anymore. New detectives, unfamiliar faces, asked him to recount the events of that day. They asked about Sam Napoli. Frankie was smart enough not to stray from the story Johnny Paradise had told reporters. *Sam Napoli was not in the restaurant.* The other patrons were so rattled that they were of no help.

One of the inquisitors did not do much talking. He was slender and thin, like his gray pencil mustache. He sat in the corner of the room, listening. After obligatory questions from obvious underlings, he rose and approached Frankie. Rather than inquire about Sam Napoli, the man asked, "How well do you know Timmy Collins?"

With the events that had played out before him, the question was beginning to make more sense. Frankie, too, was beginning to wonder: Just how well *do* I know my good friend Timmy?

* * *

Nearly half an hour later, Tracy did make her way through the emergency room. Cardio was at the nurses station, filling out paperwork. Doctors, nurses, orderlies, male and female, paused their life-saving efforts as their eyes, peeking over clipboards, followed her down the hall. She was fifteen years younger than Timmy. He had certainly picked a winner on his third try. She had a youthful, cropped hairstyle, blond, expensive, perky breasts that fought to be released from her dress, and a cashmere coat draped over her arm.

"Who did he piss off?" she asked as she came upon Cardio.

"Oh, Tracy. Good—you're here. He's been worried about you."

"Who did he piss off? I heard he was shot." She didn't sound surprised.

"No, no. It's not like that. He wasn't the target. He was just in the wrong place at the wrong time. I'll explain."

Something about her eye-roll gave Cardio the impression she didn't believe him. "Go see him. Maybe you can get him to stay overnight for observation. His blood pressure has stabilized, but still. Otherwise he's okay."

"Yeah, he needs observation all right. In a psych ward." She walked into the cubicle. "You look fine," she said.

"Tracy, Tracy—you're here," he said. "Thank you. Yes, I'm fine. It was all a misunderstanding. I was in the wrong place at the wrong . . ."

She held her hand out like a traffic cop. "Save it. It's me you're talking to. I hear the phone calls in the middle of the night. I see the men who come by to talk to you."

"No, you don't understand," he pleaded.

"Look," she said, "I'm sorry you got shot, or whatever, and there's never a good time for something like this." She took an envelope from her purse. "Or, on second thought, maybe after someone takes shots at you, this is the best time." She handed him the envelope. He opened it and read. She'd filed for a divorce in Las Vegas, where they had been married.

He felt dizzy; his hand trembled. The papers floated to the floor. "But Tracy, I thought we were going to talk about this."

"No, *you* wanted to continue talking about it. I finished talking years ago. In any case, you can come home tonight, but, until this *mishegoss* clears up, it would be best if you made arrangements to stay with one of your rat-pack friends." She turned to leave. "I do hope you get through whatever it is you're involved in."

A nurse entered as Tracy left. Tim was pale, blending into the bed linens. The monitor was beeping more quickly. "Are you all right, Mr. Collins?"

He looked at the intravenous drip. "A bag of your finest cheap cyanide," he said.

Cardio relented and agreed to sign the release. "It's against my wishes as your doctor," he said as he handed Tim his trousers and shirt. "If anything happens to you, I'll never . . ."

"What are you worried about? I'm fine." Tim assured him.

*

Chapter IX

Reno Amore, *senior investigator for the FBI*, was head of an organized-crime task force, composed of DEA, Homeland Security, ATF, and local NYPD. After a thirty-year career as a mob buster, the notches on his shield added up to a *Who's Who* of mafia crime bosses. And he wasn't finished. He had one flurry left before he retired.

Amore was a seasoned professional. He had a starchy complexion, with invisible eyebrows. He'd learned his craft as a young detective under U.S. Attorney Rudolph Giuliani. Together, they brought the Commission case. It was the first prosecution using RICO. It took down the five New York mafia families. So successful was their investigation and prosecution that the dons had put a contract out on them. That was unheard of in the annals of modern-day law enforcement. Amore was in good company. Not since New York Detective Joe Petrosino went after the Black Hand in the 1920s had a hit on a detective been ordered. The Black Hand was a precursor to the mafia. Petrosino was eventually murdered in Italy, where he was pursuing its members.

Amore's success rate was legendary. A criminal organization did not want Reno Amore on its case. With the Commission case in the history books, Amore and company were back in business. Operation New Connections sought to cripple the revitalized organized-crime families that had expanded and merged with non-traditional groups.

For the last ten years, Amore and company had been working to break the back of the Albanian mob, whose influence had grown. The Albanian mob proved to be hard to crack. New recruits to the Albanian organization were blood-related, so it was nearly impossible to plant an undercover agent. Amore was the architect who had placed Agent Sistone in the Luchese Family to the point where the agent was almost made a button-man. And, the Albanians were ruthless, making the mafia button-men seem tame by comparison. Body parts of victims would be distributed throughout the area, a trademark of the Albanian mob. Amore's investigation of the Rudaj organization spanned the tri-state area and Westchester County. Their tentacles reached all corners of the fifty states and the Middle East. The spoils from drugs and gambling had helped create a formidable criminal empire. Amore looked at the network of players. None would crack. He would need to find another way to work his way into the Rudaj, and he did.

In the early morning hours after the shooting at Johnny Paradise's Restaurant, under orders from Amore, a series of simultaneous raids took place from Bensonhurst to Palermo, from Istanbul to Staten Island. In all, sixty-two members of the Napoli, Gambino, Rudaj, and Wa Wing crime families were rounded up.

A SWAT team worthy of bin Laden encircled a quaint single-family home in Inlet Cove. Humvees were blocking the streets, and helicopters were circling above. A small army of agents, armed with tactical weapons and semi-automatic machine guns drawn, swarmed into the unassuming home, shattering the darkness. A battering ram announced their arrival as they stormed into the home to execute a warrant. A news crew from CNN was lucky enough to be set up outside the home and got the footage that would lead the news for the rest of the day and beyond. They'd been tipped off about the raid but didn't know who the target was. Reporters surmised, given the firepower, that it had to be a dangerous target, the head of an international cartel or maybe a terrorist.

Moments later, a man in a terrycloth bathrobe was led from the house, surrounded by an army of paramilitary. He was handcuffed; his legs were shackled, and his bald head was down. A woman in a sheer nightie was yelling from the door, "You really screwed the pooch this time, didn't you, Tim?"

"Bring my *toup*, and call my lawyer," he yelled back.

They escorted him into a windowless van, which was surrounded by six black Lincoln Navigators as the motorcade sped down the street.

As Tim sat inside the van on a cold, metal bench seat, a thousand calculations were going through his head. It didn't take a genius to figure things out. He leaned back. His head was spinning. He felt pins and needles in his fingers. He struggled to keep his eyes open, still groggy from medication. In a state of stupor, he assessed the situation. *Timmy Collins*, he thought, *this ain't good.*

※

Chapter X

S*am Napoli had no problem* answering questions from police. He'd had lots of practice. He was surprised, however, that Reno was involved. Reno Amore was well known to Sam. At this point, Napoli was unaware of the extent of the international raids that had taken place.

"Aren't you a little busy to be wasting your time on a rinky-dink beef? Some random kids playing with guns, from what I hear."

"Well," said Amore, "it's a slow week. I thought I'd take a ride to the country. And that gun the kid was 'playing' with," he added, "was an AK47."

Napoli was not impressed. "Whatever," he said. "In any case, there is nothing I can say." Napoli had already watched Johnny Paradise's interview on the local news. It was a smart answer. "I left the restaurant before the fuss started. I can assure you that this was not an attempt on me. Anyway, why would anyone want to kill me? I am a man of peace and go about my business as consultant to a plumbing-supply company."

Amore enjoyed the chess match with the don. The questioning was perfunctory. Not questioning the obvious target of the hit would have caused concern, and he didn't want that. He called him in, even though he knew the old don was actually telling the truth. He wasn't the target. Amore knew who was. And that target would help him put Napoli and company away and finally take down this international cabal. Timmy Collins was that link. Tim just didn't know it, yet.

*　*　*

Inwardly, the don was pissed. He'd spent his whole career in crime avoiding flamboyant displays or attracting unwanted attention. He was proud of it. He deigned the spotlight. "Never poke the bear," he'd advise his young protégés. "It makes them angry and more likely to devour you." The feds were the bear. Napoli, too, had surmised who the target was and who the trigger men were, as well as the motive. There was only one group that had no respect for tradition. Johnny Paradise and his restaurant were off limits, and any mafia crew knew that. Wise guys settling scores had best choose another venue. This could only be the Albanians. They were fearless and growing competition to the don and his old-world ways. They had no respect for boundaries, hierarchy, or chain of command. Ruthless and bloodthirsty, they made the don and his crew look like Boy Scouts, leaving a trail of body parts that kept forensic pathologists busy matching limbs to torsos. He hated doing business with them, but it had become a necessity.

Another thing that pissed him off: He had warned Timmy Collins many times: Be careful—you're playing with fire. He'd had many meetings with him and was personally invested in Tim's real-estate development business, to the point where he now controlled Tim's real-estate business. Tim proved an important asset to him in many areas. Napoli was there to assist as gambling debts rose. Tim was willing to launder money as a thank-you. His options were few. As Tim got into more trouble, the don was there to help, for a price. He learned about the arrest of his closest associates from around the world. He could understand the move by the authorities. Tim Collins was another story. Why was Timmy Collins a person of interest to Reno Amore? Tim was small time, a bit player, a useful dupe. The don concluded that Amore was starting at the bottom to get to the top. Tim Collins knew too much.

※

Chapter XI

That morning, as Frankie shaved, he listened to the news on the radio, normally white noise. But, today, something caught his ear. "The international raid that took place this morning produced a cornucopia of riches that law enforcement believes will be the final stake in the heart of organized crime." The reporter continued, "In the early-morning hours, more than sixty high-ranking *capos* from New Orleans, New York, Sicily, and Turkey were arrested. Locally, Sam Napoli, reputed boss of the Napoli crime family, and business-man Timmy Collins, a local real-estate developer, were swept up."

Blood oozed from under Frankie's ear as his razor dug in. He wiped the remnants of shaving cream from his face and fell back. Dazed and unsure that he'd heard it correctly, he stumbled to his office and found the remote. The CNN feed was being replayed on the local news. A reporter was standing on the sidewalk of a private home. It looked familiar. Then video from the actual raids splashed across the screen. He pressed a tissue on his cut. He answered the phone as he watched his friend being dragged out of his home in darkness, except for the high beams of light from a helicopter that crisscrossed the lawn. He saw Tracy yelling from the door in her nightgown.

His phone vibrated. He reached for it. "Frankie, Frankie." It was Cardio's voice.

"Cardio, are you watching?"

"Yes," Cardio said. "I just turned on the news. What the f?"

"Cardio," Frankie said, "this can't be. There must be some mistake. Some terrible mistake."

"What did we miss? How could we miss this?" Cardio responded. "Timmy, part of an international syndicate? Impossible. Impossible. It's laughable. Got to be some big mistake. Laughable, just laughable."

Absent laughter, they hung up.

❊

Chapter XII

Organized crime preys on the weak. Federal law enforcement does the same. Amore opened the folder and stared at the photograph; Exhibit 1. Timmy Collins, husband, land developer, broker, builder, degenerate gambler.

Timmy Collins sat at the federal courthouse in White Plains in a near-barren room, save a metal table and uncomfortable chairs. He tapped his fingers on the table. He had an uneasy feeling in his gut that worsened as the door opened. Reno Amore led a contingent of three other men into the room. He was holding a huge folder, and he let it fall on the desk.

"How are you, Mr. Collins?" Amore asked.

"Fine, fi . . . fi . . . fine."

"I'm Reno Amore, and you are one lucky man, it would seem," he observed.

"Yes, yes. Wrong place at the wrong time, I guess. I don't know what I can tell you. I was on the phone. I didn't see much. A van stopped, and shooting started. I dove into the bushes until it was over. I don't know what else I can say."

"Spare me, Mr. Collins." Amore opened the folder. "I know all about you. I've been studying you for sixteen months. You are in a lot of trouble, to say the least. You are bankrupt and have embezzled nearly a million dollars from your company and investors. You are up to your neck in debt, and you have no way out. And now you've pissed off the Rudaj family. They sent you a little message, didn't they?"

Collins began sweating. "I don't know what you are talking about. I was just in the wrong place. I heard something about a hit on Sam Napoli. I was minding my business."

"I'm a busy man, Collins. Let's not mince words. You lost $100K on Sunday, didn't you?" Collins was impressed, even though Amore was off by $25K. "So, they sent you a warning, didn't they?" he continued. "They don't want you dead, though. You're worth more alive. They are going to use you now for all you're worth. More land deals, Stub Hub ticket scams, mortgage fraud." He slapped his hand on the file. Collins jumped to attention. "But *I'm* going to use you first. As I see it, I've got you dead to rights on wire fraud, bank fraud, embezzlement, money laundering, brokerage fraud. You're looking at 150 years in one of our finest facilities. What are you—sixty, sixty-five? I guarantee you will rot and die in federal prison. If you think I'm bluffing, I don't bluff. Look me up. I'm Reno Amore; that's A-M-O-R-E."

Amore was making an impression. Collins felt blood draining from his face; his throat tightened—and his sphincter, too. All his assumptions had just been proven wrong. He assumed he could juggle all the competing forces. He felt certain that he'd make one big score and settle all debts. It seemed clear to him now that every step he took was being carefully monitored by the people in this room, and God knew who else was in the loop. He thought his gambling problem was his secret. He could manage it, deal with it.

"You see, Mr. Collins, it is over. Your charade is over. Your double life is over."

Collins wiped his brow. "Can I have water?" Amore motioned to grant his request. An agent put a cup in front of him.

"But," he continued, "this may be your lucky day, after all."

Collins drank; water spilled down his chin.

"You see, Mr. Collins, you are going to help me do something that I've been trying to do for years. You are going to help me crack this criminal organization." He started turning the pages in the file. One by one, he took out photographs of mobsters with whom Collins had inexplicably become involved. He was an ancillary player but one with insight and information damaging to all of them. One by one, Amore placed the photos in front of Collins. "You have unique entrée to not only the Albanian Syndicate, but the Red Tide." He held up a picture of Bobby Wong, leader of a notorious Chinese gang. "And last but not least, Vladimir Yakoff." Yakoff was head of the Russian mob, located in Bath Beach, Brooklyn. "You are at the center of four criminal organizations, a virtual United Nations of crime. Now, you are going to help me bring down Sergi, Wong, Yakoff, and Napoli. You launder money for Napoli. We know it all. You are going to wear a wire, and you are going to do all this voluntarily, to make amends for your wretched life and because you want me to recommend leniency at your sentencing. You are going to take the stand and testify about each and every one of them. If you leave anything out, I will add perjury to your crimes. And, I may even let your wife skate on being added to the indictment. I don't think she'd look good in an orange jumpsuit—not from what I saw this morning, anyway. Who knows? If all goes well, I might throw in witness protection for you and the Mrs."

Tim took a deep breath. "So, you want me to sit in a court-room and point a finger at Sam Napoli and company in return for picking potatoes in Idaho?" The thought gave him goosebumps. Plus, Tracy would never agree. She already had other plans. He fumbled with the water again. "This witness-protection thing," Timmy asked. "Would we be able to include my wife's hairdresser, trainer, and manicurist?"

Amore ignored the question. "I'm going to let you go now, Mr. Collins. I don't want to keep you any longer than others who were questioned. I don't want any red flags. If your partners in crime get suspicious, you will no longer be of value to them. It would be a shame to lose you. I'll be in touch. By the way, do you know who posted bail?"

Timmy shrugged.

"A benevolent friend," Amore said, "who wants you out on the street," he added. "I have a feeling Idaho will start looking pretty good." Amore smiled and pinched his mustache.

※

Chapter XIII

In the late afternoon on the Tuesday after the Super Bowl, Frankie Grace was examining the crime scene. Johnny, Cardio, and Nino were standing behind him, watching him move back and forth, walking off paces and examining lines of sight with extended arms. Like the fictitious detective Columbo, he seemed like a man on a mission. Something didn't sit well with him.

A section of the restaurant parking area was still cordoned off with yellow crime-scene tape. Frankie stared at the area where the bullets had hit. "Look at this." Frankie pointed to the marks. "Don't you see, guys? They're in a straight line until they get to the window where Tim was, and then they go up above the window and then down, like an arc." It wasn't registering. "Look," Frankie said. "Can you see the table where Napoli was sitting from here?"

Cardio, Johnny, and Nino looked through the window from every angle. They walked back to where tire marks showed the van stopped. The table where Napoli had been sitting was not visible.

"What are you saying?" Johnny asked.

"I'm saying I don't think this was a hit on Napoli. That's not how it would be done. A professional hit would not want ancillary casualties. I've seen it happen. Pros would have walked in the back door, done the deed, and left."

"You've seen it before?" Cardio questioned.

Frankie laughed. "I grew up on Mulberry Street. I watched the Gallo hit at Umberto's Clam House from my window."

Cardio was impressed. "So, what are you saying? If Napoli wasn't the target, who was?" There was a moment of silence until Cardio answered his own question with a question. "*Timmy?* Someone tried to kill Timmy? You don't think that this is just some crazy mistake that he got caught up in?"

"I'm just saying it doesn't make sense," Frankie said. "And besides, I don't think they wanted to kill him. If they did, they would have mowed him down without a problem. This line of bullets would have gone straight across. Instead, look at the arc."

"What then, if not kill him?" Cardio asked.

"Scare him," Frankie offered.

"We are missing something?" Johnny said. "How could we not know our best friend was into something like this? Who would want to scare him? How could he keep that from us?"

Cardio answered, "He had a secret life? That's the only conclusion. Go figure."

"Did you notice anything unusual about him lately?" Frankie asked.

"A little jumpier than usual," Cardio said.

"He borrowed $5K from me last week." Johnny's tone was matter of fact.

Cardio joined in. "I loaned him $5K, too. About three weeks ago. I didn't think anything of it."

"Wow." Frankie scratched his head.

"Don't tell me you loaned him $5K, too," Cardio said, looking at Frankie.

"Of course not," Frankie assured them. A moment later, he added, "I loaned him $10K."

The men looked at each other. "You know, it makes sense," Frankie continued. "Those detectives running around the hospital. They asked me more questions about Tim than about Napoli."

"That federal guy, with the mustache, tried to corner me, too," Cardio reported. "I brushed him off, but he showed up in my office today. He scared the crap out of me. Wanted to know what I saw. Kept pressing me about Sammy and Tim. But you're right: he asked a lot of questions about Tim."

"Have you heard from Tim?" Johnny asked.

"Not since he was released," Cardio said.

Now, they knew why.

✳

Chapter XIV

As *Cardio and Frankie waited* for Timmy to arrive, they sat listening to Nino. The conversation took their mind off their worries about their friend, as Nino was explaining the concept of the clinic in Sicily. "It's all built around the thermal spring waters from the caverns of San Calogero," he explained. "The springs have wonderful medicinal benefits. Add to that the use of ozone gas mixed with one's blood in a centrifuge, and you're giving renewed energy and youthfulness to clients. There is an intravenous injection for every malady. It's all about platelet-rich plasma. Princes and princesses, the glitterati from all over Europe, are among our valued clientele." Judging from the blank looks on their faces, he determined they were not impressed.

As a local carpenter repaired the shelving behind the bar, Johnny was on the phone. "Table for two, eight o'clock. I got it," he said. He scratched his mustache and tapped the pencil on the podium. The shooting, along with the news coverage and his statement, was being played and replayed on every news cycle on every station. It was picked up by Fox, ABC, and CBS, and it went nationwide, as it was tied to the sweeping international raids that had taken place. Thanks to Tim Collins, Inlet Cove and Paradise's Italian Restaurant were on the map.

Johnny's instinct told him something strange was going on. "That was the third call for reservations," he shared the news. "It seems there is no such thing as bad publicity when it comes to advertising. I couldn't buy this." He tossed a copy of the local news on the table. The restaurant was on the front page. The carpenter removed his father's portrait for repair. "Hold up," Johnny ordered. "Leave the old man up there, as is." The carpenter obliged, placing the portrait back on the wall. "Hey," he said to the carpenter, "on second thought, do me a favor. Make that hole a little bigger. Use a screwdriver or something. Just a little bigger."

"You're a marketing genius," Cardio observed. Johnny winked and gave a thumbs-up, acknowledging the compliment.

Try as they might to show interest in Nino and his business, their mind was somewhere else. Each wondered out loud how they could have missed it. Could Timmy have a side to him that his best friends were unaware of? How could they not know? What they were hearing, reading about their friend? Impossible.

"Did anybody see this?" Cardio asked.

"I knew he made a few bets," Johnny said. "Football sheets, pools, and such. Nothing serious."

All conversation stopped as Timmy, or a version of Timmy, entered the restaurant. There was no bounce in his step, no song on his lip, and no cigar dangling from his fingertip. He was worn out; two days of growth darkened his face. His eyes were puffy, his hair un-coiffed. Johnny brought a bottle of wine to the table as Frankie and Cardio rushed to his side. There was utter silence until Frankie asked, "Timmy, what the f?"

Timmy fell into a chair. His head fell into his arms, crossed on the table. "Guys," he said, "I'm sorry. I'm so screwed, so screwed. But it's not what you think. I'm not in any syndicate or anything like that."

"What do you mean, Timmy?" Cardio asked.

"It's over. My life is over. Marco, I need something stronger. A bottle of his best cheap whiskey."

Marco brought a bottle of Bushmills. "I'm Catholic," Timmy objected. "Jameson—get the Jameson."

Timmy raised his head long enough to down a shot of whiskey. His friends just looked at each other, lost for anything to say. Cardio finally asked, "What's going on, Timmy?"

"I'm a fraud," he said. "I've been living a lie."

"What are you talking about, Timmy?" Frankie asked.

"Guys, I'm an addict. I have a gambling addiction, and I'm so screwed. It's over. My life is over. There—I've said it. It's out there."

"*A gambling addiction?* What do you mean? When did this start?" Frankie asked.

"I don't know. High school, I guess."

"An addiction?" Cardio asked. "Maybe you just had a bad day."

"No, I've had bad *years*. Kept getting worse and worse, deeper and deeper. I'm involved with some very bad people."

"And do we know these people?" Frankie asked.

"No, no," Tim explained. "I'd never let you guys know about those guys. It's embarrassing. Now you know. I'm a degenerate. I tried to balance two worlds, but it's crashing down now. Suffice to say, I'm screwed."

"Easy," Johnny said. "If it's money, we can help straighten you out."

"Money won't solve it, even if you had enough. I'm up to my neck with people I don't even know who have devoured my soul. I'm a thief. I've embezzled from my investors. I took escrow deposits on the Pineridge Development. I conspired with Napoli. I thought it would be a temporary loan. The banks were foreclosing. I had to borrow from people I shouldn't have. I cooked the books to show collateral. It's over for me. I'm into the Albanians, the Russians, and the Chinese. Not to mention the mafia. Now, with this arrest, I can only imagine what my life is worth. To make matters worse, the feds want me to wear a wire and testify. When that word gets out, I'm dead. I'm looking at a hundred years in prison. In a federal prison with Albanians and Chinese and Italians all looking to make their mark. I'm screwed. I'm dead. Either way, I'm finished. If I help the feds or not. I've screwed myself really good. I wish I were dead. I'm worth more dead than alive, anyway. It's the only way out. I wish I were dead."

The four men were shocked. Timmy's hand was shaking. He downed another shot. They all followed his cue, wrestling with the confession they'd just heard. Cardio was like a zombie, staring into space. He took off his glasses and rubbed his eyes. "Are you saying those bullets were meant to kill you? Then Frankie was right?" Cardio asked.

Frankie responded, "Not *kill* him. I'd say *scare the crap* out of him."

Tim picked his head up and nodded. "Yes, it was meant to scare me. I owe them so much that they want me to continue with this scam that rakes in millions. They buy tear-down houses. I up the appraisal, so they get a big mortgage. Then they walk away, leaving the bank holding the bag on worthless property. So, you see, I'm dead either way. Dead, dead, dead."

Frankie circled the table, scratching his head. Johnny and Nino fiddled with silverware. Sorrowful moans emanated from Timmy. With his head nestled in his folded arms, he said again, "Dead—I wish I were dead. They want me to sit in a courtroom and point the finger at Napoli and a dozen other guys. They offered witness protection. I'll never make it that far. I can't go down that road. It's not in my DNA, which is composed of chickenshit. I wish I could start over, with a clean slate, but I'm too far gone."

Frankie understood the gravity of the situation better than most. His education had taken place on the streets of Manhattan, where, as a young man, he'd had his own dealings with "made men," feds, crooks, and creeps. He'd gotten himself in trouble a long time ago and understood that these people do not fool around. All those memories came back to him. If not for a good friend, he may well have been buried in a landfill on Staten Island. Now it may be the time for him to be the good friend, to return the favor.

Timmy's voice was muffled, his head still resting on his arms. "I wish I were dead," was the chant as he lifted his head up repeatedly and banged it down again on the table.

It was then that Frankie stopped walking. His eyes widened, and he seemed possessed. "What if you were?" Frankie asked.

Timmy did not raise his head. Muffled, he uttered, "Were what?"

"Dead," the undertaker said.

Cardio, Johnny, and Nino stared at Frankie. Even old man Paradise, hanging behind the bar, appeared to raise an eyebrow.

Frankie walked around the table, mumbling more than speaking.

"Frankie, what are you saying? Speak up," Johnny said.

"I'm trying to think out of the box. That's all."

"Did he just say that?" Johnny asked.

"He did," Cardio confirmed.

"Guys, I'm thinking about him," Frankie said, pointing to Tim. "About being dead as his only out. About a clean slate, a second chance to start over."

"I'm sure it was just an expression," Cardio observed. "Wasn't it?"

Frankie took a seat. "Listen, I'm just thinking out loud. We are looking at a dead man one way or another. If he cooperates with the feds or doesn't, he's dead. The mob won't take a chance. He's a liability, and they will cut their losses. We, on the other hand, may have the ability to grant his wish."

Timmy lifted his head long enough to ask, "Who is this guy?" referring to Frankie.

"Why couldn't it happen? Frankie insisted. "His death would make this whole thing go away."

"Is anyone hearing what I'm hearing?" Timmy asked.

"What do you think?" Frankie said, ignoring him. "Do you think it could work? Do you think we can find a way to kill off our friend and get him a fresh start?"

"So, you're proposing we fake Tim's death. *Poof*, he's gone." Johnny wiped his hands together like Pontius Pilate. "Dying from natural causes might piss off some people," he observed.

Cardio downed a shot. His interest had been piqued. "Basically," he mused, "getting rid of him is only half the problem. We'd also have to get him a new identity, which is more common than you might imagine."

"Yeah," Frankie agreed. "We're doing both. We find a way to fake his death. We get him a new identity, and he gets a new start. It's our version of a witness-protection program."

"It would be a long shot," Johnny said. "It would take a lot of planning; there are a lot of unknowns."

"You said it," Cardio added. "Plus, there is liability. Laws will be broken, careers ruined, and prison in our future should it fail." Then he added, "Just crazy enough to work. Crazier things have been done. We've really got to think it through. Anyway, it'll give us something to do."

"I don't believe this," Timmy said, looking at the doctor. "You're the smart one. You're supposed to be the realistic one. Even though you went to medical school in Costa Rica, I thought you'd be smarter than to think this is a good idea."

"Grenada," he corrected him. "I'm just trying to save your life. If you have a better idea, let's hear it. It's just theoretical right now, just brainstorming."

Over the next few minutes, Frankie expounded on his idea. "Listen," Frankie said. "We have all the ingredients. I'm a funeral director, and you're a doctor."

"Supposedly," Timmy said. The remark was met with Cardio's middle finger, as was the usual practice.

"Will you ever stop breaking my balls?" he asked.

"It's only because I love ya," Tim answered. "But I can't believe that you're buying into this crazy idea."

"What's so crazy?" Frankie asked. "A doctor is all you need to be declared dead, and, if he's in cahoots with the undertaker, it's all the easier to accomplish."

The idea he was suggesting—and his reasoning for it—flowed out of Frankie as naturally as wine flowed in. His friends exchanged incredulous glances. The idea was so fluid that Johnny had to ask, "Have you done this before?" Frankie didn't answer.

"Are you proposing I pronounce him dead and issue a death certificate?" Cardio asked.

"And I will provide a funeral—that's on me," Frankie said.

"And I guess I provide the body," Tim added.

"It's the least you can do," Johnny said.

Johnny sat down next to Timmy. He put his arm around his shoulder. "First, you have to answer one question. Are you ready to give it all up? Leave it all? Trade everything you have, which is nothing, give up all the people you know, the places you know, the things you know—and disappear, never to return?" The options, as laid out before him, were bleak. "Do you think you'd be able to leave Tracy?" Johnny added.

Timmy laughed. He took an envelope out of his pocket and handed it to Johnny.

Johnny opened it and read. "Holy Jesus," he said. He passed the letter around the table.

"This answers one part of your question," Tim said. "Tracy filed for divorce. She's leaving me."

"Christ, how long has this been going on?" Johnny asked. "I had no idea."

"A long time. I think she's been cheating on me. We've been cohabitating but not co-fornicating. I brought a lot of stress to her life. She couldn't take it. Now this. It was too much."

Frankie saw a practical problem with this development. "Now, she can testify against you, and you know they will get her to flip."

That deserved another round of Jameson.

"So," Johnny said, "if we were making a list of pros and cons on should we or shouldn't we, this would be on the pro side. It's not like you are leaving the love of your life behind."

"Still, you guys, my life . . ." Tim lamented.

"If not," Frankie reminded him, "we can visit you once a month or so, depending on where you're imprisoned."

Johnny chimed in, "But that will be only for a year or so." Everyone looked at him. "He'll be dead in a year," Johnny explained. "A fight in the yard, or found in his cell with a make-shift knife in his heart, or hanging by his own bed sheets. It'll happen, no doubt. It'll be ruled a suicide." The men were quiet as those words sunk in.

Frankie appreciated Johnny's view. If he doubted Johnny's credentials, he need only look behind the bar, where Paradise senior's ventilated portrait was hanging.

Timmy swallowed hard. His hands shook.

"I don't think you have a choice," Cardio observed.

"Oh, Christ, what do I do? What do I do now? Where will I go?"

"You can come home with me," Nino offered.

"I don't have all the answers," Frankie admitted. "As Cardio said, we've got to think it through. Between us, we will cover all the bases. I say we proceed. We take it one step at a time. If, at any point, we want to throw in the towel, if something goes wrong, if we're not comfortable or change our mind, we end it. No questions asked; no harm, no foul. We'll say we tried and move on. That goes for any one of us. We are all in or all out."

"We may not have a lot of time," Johnny said.

Frankie sat at the table and poured another drink. "Come to my office tomorrow," he said.

"For what?" Timmy asked.

"You need to make your funeral arrangements. That would be the first step. You have to have plans on file. Your wife, soon to be ex-wife, will still have to sign off on it. She's still your nearest relative. Then we will have to get you a new identity to replace the one that's dead. That would be the second step. Without that, we are just spinning our wheels."

❄

Chapter XV

Timmy did not sleep well. He fidgeted all evening in the recliner in his office. Tracy made it clear he'd be sleeping there for the foreseeable future. In any case, he didn't want to put her in harm's way. More "messages" might be in the works. He heard cars stopping outside his window at all hours. The script Cardio wrote to relax him wasn't working. As far as the idea that Frankie had come up with, he wondered if that could even work. And, if it did, would he be able to be on the lam for the rest of his life? Leave all the people, places and things he knew, just as Johnny had so clearly explained it. His options were few and none good. Prison was a death sentence, anyway. Johnny was right about that, too. There were people who wanted him dead, and it would be a résumé boost to deliver his corpse to the guards on duty. Being fake dead as opposed to real dead was beginning to look a lot better. With great trepidation and reservations, he followed Frankie's instructions.

He'd known Frankie for more than thirty years, but he knew only a little about his life before he'd come to Westchester. Knowing he came from Little Italy in New York, it made some kind of sense that this idea would spring from his mind so quickly. He was more surprised at Cardio. The good doctor was not prone to risk. He was more an eater than a drinker, although Timmy noted he had downed a few that afternoon. Still, risking his license to practice medicine—and jail time as well? Some part of him hoped Cardio would be the voice of reason, explaining why this plan would not, could not work. Instead the normally practical doctor drank a second and third and nodded, saying, "Just crazy enough to work. Stranger things have happened."

※

Chapter XVI

Following Frankie's instructions, Timmy drove to the funeral home. He brought his passport, again as instructed. In the basement of the funeral home, there was a showroom for caskets, an outer office for meeting with families, and, beyond another door was the embalming room. Timmy took a seat; Frankie had a file ready. "I'm going to predate this, as if you'd made these arrangements a while ago. When did Cardio send you to have the stents put in?"

Timmy thought for a moment. "Fifteen," he said, "June 3, 2015."

"Good," Frankie said. He put a date of May 30 on the file. "It will make sense when it hits the fan that you made prearrangements when you were dealing with your heart issue. Getting affairs in order and all that."

"What do my affairs have to do with anything?" Timmy asked.

Frankie continued. "Not that kind of affair, you mook." Tim nodded. Frankie continued, "I need to know your mother's and father's name."

"For what?" Timmy asked.

"Your death certificate. In order to get permits, I'll have to file a death certificate."

"This is weird," Timmy said. "James and Margaret," he added.

"How about your mother's maiden name and Tracy's? I'll need hers, too."

"Shea and Schwartz, in that order." Frankie smirked. Timmy stood up and started walking around the office. He opened a door and peeked into the casket showroom. It contained eighteen caskets, in all price ranges. "I remember picking out my mom's casket in here, like it was yesterday." He walked into the room, admiring them. He ran his hand across the velvet interior and knocked on the lids. He stopped at a solid bronze unit with a full, open, one-piece glass lid and a plush tufted-velvet interior. "This one's for me," he said. "Top shelf. I'll take this one."

"It won't work," Frankie said without looking up.

"Why? It's the best. I always went first class. I'm not changing now."

"Because it won't burn, idiot. You're being cremated."

"Cremated!" The word did not sit well with the Irish Catholic.

"Timmy, don't you understand? There can be no trace of you."

"Cremated," Timmy repeated. "How will I explain it to my mother?"

"She's dead," he reminded him.

"Jesus, Frankie—I don't know about this." Timmy was confused. There was a cardboard box in the corner. "I'm not going in a cardboard casket," he said. "I have some standards. I don't want to look like a cheapskate."

"God forbid," Frankie said. He finished taking the vital statistical information needed to file the future death certificate.

"I have a question," Tim said. "It's delicate. How should I handle my first two wives? Should they get an honorary mention in my obituary or not mentioned at all?"

"I'll get back to you on that. Let me think," Frankie said.

Tim nodded. "I don't want to piss Tracy off any more than I have already. Although, it's not like she'll be able to yell at me."

"There are more important issues right now. I have to figure out the wake," Frankie said. He leaned back in his chair. "It won't fly to announce you've died. We will have to prove it. We will need to have one evening wake, a few hours. Just how to do that, I have to figure out. It can't be a memorial without your body present or simply an urn in the room. That won't fly. It won't satisfy the interested parties."

"I need more than a few hours. I've got lots of friends. People will be coming from out of town. I need three days, minimum."

"Are you out of your mind? Don't you understand what we're planning? Three days? One ladies' night, Karaoke, drinks half price? It's a *wake*—to let your enemies know that you're dead and they don't have to kill you anymore."

"I guess you're right. I don't think I could lie still that long, anyway."

Frankie hadn't gotten around to figuring out that part. It was a work in progress. Timmy was jumpy, fidgeting, pacing. Watching him do the St. Vitus dance, Frankie doubted he could get him to lie still for three minutes, never mind three hours.

Frankie just shrugged. "You don't get it, do you? It's important that all your enemies see you in the casket. Or at least think it's you in the casket," he said as an afterthought. "After that, I can bring you to the crematory. They will probably follow. I have to figure that out. Right now, I'm thinking of a mannequin or something. I've got to think."

Timmy was still focused on the ritual. "No funeral mass? Bad enough I'm being cremated, but now I'm not having a mass! I'll go straight to hell."

"Did you think heaven was in the cards? Mass or no mass, I think hell is your more likely destination." Tim raised his middle finger. Frankie smiled. "Let me think; just let me think."

Timmy objected to being brought to the crematory after the visitation. "Frankie, you got to understand. I'm Catholic. I should have a funeral mass at St. Catherine's with an organist and singer. I'm sure someone will want to say something nice, maybe Cardio or even Tracy. We had something special once. I think. I'll write some bullet points to remind her."

"*Bullet* being the operative word," Frankie said.

"You're a funny man," Tim said. He tapped his finger on the desk. "I must have a mass. Otherwise I'll go straight to hell. And it wouldn't be right if someone didn't say something nice about me."

"If you want something nice said, you'll have to write it yourself."

Tim nodded. "I can do that."

※

Chapter XVII

*E*ven Frankie was unsure of every detail. He hoped that there would be a solution to each roadblock, that solutions would reveal themselves as obstacles arose. "First things first," as he explained to Timmy and Cardio. "It all begins with a new identity," Frankie said.

Timmy got into Frankie's Audi. "Where are we headed?"

"We are going downtown, to Mulberry Street."

"What's there?"

"If this is going to work, we will need help. I have a good friend who might be able to get us started."

Timmy sat back. "Mulberry Street. Wow! It must have been great growing up there." Timmy was a mob groupie. He'd watched *The Godfather* countless times and had chosen its theme song, "Speak Softly, Love," as his wedding song—all three times.

"Yeah, it was a great place to grow up. You really got an education, and I don't mean from books."

"So, who are we going to see?" Tim asked.

"My friend Eddie Fontana. He's like an older brother to me. My parents took him in and put a roof over his head. He was seemingly slow-witted, and everyone called him 'Special Ed.' As it turned out, he wasn't so slow, after all. He actually saved my life, and by a series of events, he became the boss of the Ballsziti crime family."

"Ballsziti, really? They're big. I read about them all the time. I follow them on my Gangland account. That Capeci reporter is fearless. He knows where all the bodies are buried."

"Yep. So did I."

"You actually know the head of the Ballsziti family. You never mentioned it. Wow!"

"I guess there's a lot about me you don't know. Dare say there was a lot about you that fooled me."

"At the end of the day, does anyone ever know anyone?" Tim asked.

"How profound," Frankie said.

Timmy resigned himself to the observation. "And you say this 'Eddie' guy was not so smart."

"Well, there was something about him. For all his shortcomings, he had a certain savant ability to play chess. And he was good-hearted, a real character. He dressed in colorful untucked bowling shirts. He had them in all colors, and the weather did not matter. It was his trademark. He got me out of a few jams and protected me like an older brother. He was a gofer of sorts for Ballsziti—small jobs, errands—and then graduated to enforcement when needed."

"You mean muscle?"

"Yes. By happenstance, he became head of the family when Ballsziti got pinched by the feds. With the help, might I add, of the seemingly slow-witted Special Ed."

"So this Eddie set up his boss to save your life? Tell me how."

Frankie was reluctant to talk too much, but he saw no harm in revealing some of his ancient adventures.

"Well, I got involved with Ballsziti thinking he could help further my career in showbusiness. I wanted to be a stand-up comedian when I was young, but my father wouldn't hear of it. My father was a serious man. He never laughed. Comedy and mortician did not mix. Anyway, without my father knowing and with the help of Ballsziti, I got some gigs."

"You really did it? Stand-up? I thought you were kidding. So, why did you give it up?"

"For one thing, I wasn't funny. Then my father died, and I just couldn't walk away from his business. I couldn't close the doors. I operated the small place for a few years and then made the move to Westchester when I bought the funeral home. Stand-up was a teenage pipedream. Anyway, it was a lifetime ago."

Timmy was intrigued. "I can't believe I didn't know this about you."

"Listen, Timmy: How many years have I known you?"

Timmy thought for a moment. "At least thirty-five years. You buried my mother and then my father a year later."

"Well, I had a life before I got to Westchester."

"So, tell me, how did this 'Eddie' guy save your life?"

Frankie thought hard about how much to reveal. "Well, any favor comes with a price," he explained. "Along the way, I got involved with Ballsziti's daughter, and things got pretty intense. Ballsziti was not happy with that. Then he asked me for a favor—*insisted* more than asked. Anyway, I helped Ballsziti smuggle cash stolen from the Federal Reserve Bank to Italy in his mother-in-law's casket. I'm not proud of it, but you don't say 'No' to these people, not at my age and not if you planned on getting older. Between that and the fact that I knew where some bodies were buried, word was there was a contract out on me. Ballsziti wanted me out of his daughter's life, and I was a witness to the smuggling. My disappearance would be a win-win for him. That's where Eddie came to my rescue." Frankie left out the fact that Eddie had been ordered to make the hit. That request got him to turn on his boss.

"Jesus," Timmy said, "talk about not knowing a guy. I had no idea you were so involved. Wow, there was a contract on you. My friend Frankie could have been whacked. I would have never known you. Wow! I can't believe you have that kind of past. I'm impressed."

"It wasn't all that glamorous, believe me."

He reached for the phone buzzing in his pocket. "Yes, dear. Hello," he said into the phone. "The sprinkler isn't working? Maybe it's the timer . . . did you check?" He listened. "Sometimes a little lightning strike can make that happen. Okay, okay—you check, or call the landscaper . . . no, I don't have his number. Okay, okay. I'll call you later."

Timmy was deep in thought. "Wow," he said again. "And the girl, what happened to the girl? The Ballsziti chick?"

Frankie put the phone back into his pocket. "I married her," he said.

❊

Chapter XVIII

The panoramic granite vista of Manhattan Island lay before them as Frankie drove along the Brooklyn Queens Expressway toward the Williamsburg Bridge. Across the East River, the Chrysler and Empire State Buildings, and the Freedom Tower to the south framed the island. He had made this trip countless times, mostly to visit his mother, who insisted on staying in the same apartment where she'd lived her whole life. It is where she wanted to die. She got her wish and, up to that point, he visited three times a week.

He drove along Delancey to Mott and pulled into a garage. A Chinese man handed him a ticket. "Thirty-five dollar," he said.

"Jesus," Timmy remarked. "We don't want the oil changed."

"Thirty-five dollar," he said again.

Frankie stepped onto the sidewalk and took a deep breath as he stared up and down the street. There was something distinctly different in his old neighborhood. Even Timmy noticed.

"This is Little Italy?" he asked.

"It was," Frankie answered. He understood Timmy's question, for, as far as the eye could see, there were no Italians. The mom-and-pop restaurants were gone. The mélange of aromas emanating from the former *trattorias* was different. Sauces and meats that were prepared in the dozens of Italian restaurants along Mulberry Street had been replaced by Asian fusion, Thai, Szechuan, and Mandarin. It had been years since he'd last visited, and he was stunned as he walked down the street.

He stopped by a building. On the wall of a building, behind a cart filled with bok choy, there was a plaque. "This was our funeral home," he explained to Timmy. Timmy read the plaque. "At this location, from 1912 to 1980, The Grace Funeral Home was owned and operated by the Grace Family. The matriarch, Maddie Grace, lived in the three-room apartment on the first floor until her death."

Timmy was incredulous. "This is where you grew up? Are you sure? It's a Chinese vegetable store."

Frankie felt a pain in his heart.

He pointed to other storefronts. Not a *cannoli* to be found. The change that prompted his move to Inlet Cove years earlier was complete. The five-story walk-up tenements were the same, untouched by modernity, but the character was different, as the hustle and commerce were in Chinese hands. Featherless ducks took the place of *prosciuttos* hanging in the windows of the butcher shops. Italian cafes and pastry shops gave way to teahouses. Nail salons, tantric-massage parlors, and Chinese acupuncture with competing sandwich-board advertisements blocked the sidewalks, replacing pasta shops, Italian novelties, and music stores.

"Hey, we could probably get a massage with a happy ending down here."

"At your age," Frankie answered, "a happy ending is if they don't steal your wallet."

Frankie wondered if he would even find his old friend Eddie in the Italian café where he'd made his headquarters. He stopped in front of a building near Mott Street. "It was here," he said. "I'm sure the café was here." Now, the small storefront was occupied by Ciao Mein Chinese Restaurant. Two expressionless oriental men stood, like lions, guarding the entrance. Frankie scratched his head in disbelief.

He approached them. "Excuse me, would you happen to know what happened to the man who used to own this?"

One of the men asked, "Who wants to know?"

"I'm an old friend of his. My name is Frankie; his name is Eddie."

One man walked into the restaurant. Moments later, he returned and waved them forward. Timmy followed Frankie through the entrance, moving a curtain of plastic beads that were strung above the door. They clicked as they came through, an abacus-style alarm system. He adjusted his eyes to the darkness and stared at the man in the corner. It was Eddie. He was surrounded by three other men, and there was a game board on the table with black and white pieces. Eddie stopped playing and dismissed the men, waving Frankie forward. Timmy started to follow until Eddie put up a single finger.

"Stay here," Frankie said. "Just sit here."

As Frankie approached, Eddie stood up and held out his arms. "My brother, my brother. How are you? How long has it been?"

Frankie embraced Eddie and kissed his cheek. He sat down and tried to wrap his head around the surroundings. In a small alcove, there was a miniature Buddha with a lit votive candle at its base. It sat on the shelf once occupied by a statue of San Gennaro, the patron saint of Naples. Eddie noticed him looking at it. "Hey," he said, "when in Rome . . ." Frankie nodded. Eddie had aged. His complexion was gaunt, ghostlike, contrasting against the dark surroundings. His hair had thinned, hardly enough for a comb-over, and a tooth was missing. His trademark shirt had been replaced by an elegant burgundy Oriental silk jacket with colorful songbirds sitting on a branch embroidered on its chest.

"About eighteen years, I'd say, give or take," Eddie said, answering his own question, his voice interrupting the darkness.

Frankie settled back into the chair. "Yeah, exactly," he agreed. "After my mother died, I just lost it. I just lost it. I couldn't bring myself to . . ."

"To visit old friends." Eddie finished the sentence.

"It wasn't that," Frankie said.

"You don't have to explain. I miss your mother every day. She was a good woman. Your father, I miss him, too. A pain in the ass, but, in the end, he was a stand-up guy. I know you've been doing well up there in the country. I understand. Would you like some tea?" A porcelain teapot was brought to the table. Eddie poured tea into a demitasse cup.

Frankie smiled. "Tea?" he asked. "You were good for a dozen espressos back in the day."

Eddie sipped, explaining, "It made me too tense, but again, 'When in Rome.' Try the *oolong*—very relaxing."

"The place has certainly changed," Frankie said. "I hardly recognize it. *Ciao Mein*?"

"Clever, right? My idea," Eddie said. "Yes, I changed a few things around. I had a Feng Shui expert come in to help me get just the right feel. It promotes harmony and inner peace, good karma and all that stuff."

Frankie nodded and stared at the game board. "No more chess?" he asked. For all his seeming lack of mental acumen, Eddie had a penchant for chess.

"Ah," Eddie said, "no, this is Go. It's a hundred times more challenging than chess. An ancient Chinese game. Chess is played on the right side of the brain; it's tactical. GO requires both sides of your brain. It's patterns and tactical."

Frankie nodded. "I know—'When in Rome.'"

"What about Lucci? Do you hear from that slug?" Sal Lucci was another friend from back in the day.

"I do. He calls once a month or so. He's in Nevada promoting rock bands and wrestlers or something."

"I know. I got him out of a jam. Not the first, either."

Frankie smiled and nodded that he understood. "Probably not the last."

"Well, Frankie, my brother. We had some good days. Dodged a bullet here and there, literally." He laughed. Frankie did, too. "Of course, you know he's dead. Johnny Ballsziti is dead. I thought the bastard would live forever. What was he, ninety?"

"Ninety-eight," Frankie said. "I thought it would take a stake in the heart to kill him."

Eddie smiled. "Yeah, you don't have to be afraid to call him 'Johnny Balls' anymore. Remember how you used to get tongue tied around him? He made you so nervous. He didn't like that nickname."

"He sure did make me nervous. Obviously, I had to take care of his funeral arrangements. I had his body brought from Marion and had him cremated."

Eddie sipped his tea and chuckled. "I didn't think you could burn shit."

Frankie laughed, too. "And his daughter—how is she?"

"Fine," Frankie said. "She's in Florida for the winter. I go back and forth."

Eddie nodded. "Hey, what kind of host am I? Would you like some Dim Sum, something to eat? Some Lo Mein? You know the Chinese invented spaghetti."

"No, no. I'm fine."

"So, my brother, what can I do for you? To what do I owe this visit?"

"I need help," Frankie said.

"Are you in trouble?"

"No, not me." He motioned to his friend. Timmy was sitting at a table by the door, playing with his fingernails. Sunlight coming through the window engulfed his head in a halo.

"Is he one of us?" he asked.

"No, Irish," Frankie answered apologetically.

Eddie nodded. "What's that thing on his head?"

They both stared at Timmy. "A hairpiece," Frankie answered.

Eddie's eyebrows went up, and his lips pursed. "He looks like a chooch," he said. Both men nodded. "So, what can I do for you? What is the nature of your request?"

"He's in big trouble. He got himself mixed up with Albanians and Chinese gangs and is being squeezed by the feds. He's in a vise."

Eddie nodded. "You stick your neck out for this guy. You vouch for him?"

"I do," Frankie said. "I do."

"And how can I help? What can I do? I can sit down with these people . . . get them to back off."

Frankie shook his head, explaining it was too far gone. If the Albanian score was settled, there were the Russians, and, of course, the feds were relentless. "He's facing a hundred years for his crimes," Frankie explained. "He's also in trouble with Sam Napoli."

"Napoli?" Eddie said. "This guy gets around." Frankie nodded. Eddie shrugged. "What then?"

Frankie leaned in and whispered as Eddie listened, nodding every few seconds. He smiled, at one point observing, "And I thought you left the neighborhood. I guess you can take the boy out of Mulberry Street, but you can't take Mulberry Street out of the boy. I like your idea. It reminds me of the old days. Remember some of the things we did? Remember the cash we smuggled to Italy in Mrs. Cianci's casket?" Eddie laughed until he coughed.

"I sure do."

"So, what can I do to help?"

"The first thing I need is to get him a new identity. He will have to leave New York, maybe even the country. Maybe Italy."

"So, he needs paperwork?" Eddie asked. He nodded, and then he leaned into Frankie and whispered. Frankie walked to Timmy and asked for his passport, returning to the table with it. He did not hand it to Eddie. He just left it on an empty chair at the table.

"You knew I'd help you, didn't you?" Eddie said.

"Well, let's say, I was hoping."

"Give me a week," Eddie said.

"I can't thank you enough. Just tell me how much I owe . . ." He stopped in mid-sentence as Eddie's eyes commanded.

"Your mother and father were like my own," Eddie said. "He was a pain in the ass, but he was a stand-up guy. Helped Ballsziti in the old days with a double-decker casket now and then. This is not about money, my brother. This is about friendship. When it all comes down, friendship is all we have."

Frankie rose and kissed Eddie again. Before turning away, he embraced him and felt a rush of emotion as his whole past came pouring through. His eyes welled up. Eddie held him at arm's length, his hands firm on his shoulder. "Do you know what you are doing?" he asked. "You sure you vouch for this guy? You built a good life for yourself. Are you ready to risk it at your age for . . . an Irishman?" He had to ask.

Frankie wiped his eyes and nodded "Yes." Eddie patted his cheek again. "Come back in a week," he said again. Frankie turned to leave and then turned back.

"Eddie, what happened to this neighborhood? What happened to Little Italy?"

Eddie was wistful, melancholy. Light from decorative colored lanterns strung across the ceiling reflected on his silk jacket, bathing him in soft hues. His hands firmly clasped behind his back, he shrugged.

"The *paisanos* became *Taiwanos*," he said.

❄   ❄   ❄

As instructed, Timmy sat in a chair by the door. Eddie was a careful man, not about to trust this Irishman who needed his help. He left himself plausible deniability should the whole plan fail—the possibility of which he handicapped at sixty-forty, against. But together they had done worse.

As he saw the meeting end, Timmy rose, not knowing whether to approach, shake hands, kiss, hug. He stood feebly by the door, and, as Frankie approached, he simply waved to Eddie. The gesture was not returned.

As they walked back to the car, both of them felt out of place. They stood out like brown shoes with a black tuxedo. A thousand Chinese eyes made only cursory contact. They were the invaders. Pedestrians hustled past them. They were of no interest to the new occupants of the former Little Italy. It was not so for the FBI surveillance team that sat crammed into a FedEx truck a short distance away. The team of agents monitored, on a daily basis, the comings and goings at Eddie Fontana's Ciao Mein Restaurant. By the time they began walking, facial-recognition technology had identified Frankie Grace and Timmy Collins. A red light blinked over Collins' computer image.

With the big granite island fading in the background, Timmy sat back. "How did it go?" he asked. "Can he help?"

"Yes. I knew he would. We got to go back in a week. You'll have a new identity."

"What then?"

"I'm not quite sure. Gotta think."

Timmy was quiet. "So, you should know. What do you think happens after you die?"

Frankie looked at him. "Where did that come from?"

"Just wondering. Thought you might know."

"Nothing," Frankie said.

"I mean, do you think there's heaven, hell, purgatory?"

"No," Frankie said. "I think when you die, you die. It's over. No heaven, no hell."

"Jesus, that's depressing."

"Don't sweat it. You'll never know, anyway."

"I didn't think you were so cynical."

Frankie shrugged. "I've been burying people my whole life. I've come to the conclusion that death changes everything and changes nothing. Life goes on for everyone, eventually. You die; then you become a memory, then a faded memory, and then, any memory of you is actually a memory of the faded memory."

"Jesus, that's cold."

"Just my observation," Frankie said. "I guess I am cynical. I've been acquainted with grief my whole life. People crying, mourning, saying goodbye. It gets to you, dealing with death daily."

"Well, I think you're wrong. Tracy will be inconsolable. She'll miss me when I'm gone—you'll see. She'll be sorry she filed for divorce. I'm sure of it. My Tracy. I'm doing this for her, too. With me gone, she'll be safe. She won't be dragged into the investigation by the feds or the retaliation by the mob."

"That's the idea," Frankie agreed.

Timmy nodded. "Then again, when she finds out the house is mortgaged to the max and I went through all our savings . . ." he paused. "Let's just say I'll be glad I'm already dead. When she gets mad, she can scare the balls off a pool table. I really got myself mixed up in a mess."

"Yes, you did."

"I was wondering, you being the professional and all, did you give any thought to the obituary? How would you handle my first two wives?"

"Is this really a pressing issue?"

"Well, I don't want to hurt anyone's feelings."

"You're kidding, right?"

"I mean, should they get mentioned? Should I acknowledge them? Or let sleeping dogs lie? I don't want to hurt anyone's feelings. They're already pissed at me." That got a look from Frankie.

"What's the story with them, anyway? What broke up your first marriage?"

Tim stretched his legs. "Talk about sleeping dogs. It was a Yorkie, a damn Yorkie named Gulliver. Liz loved that dog."

"What happened?"

"She went to visit her mother for a few days. I was taking care of the mutt. He was a yapper; yap, yap, yap. Anyway, I took care of him, walked him, fed him. One night I'm out drinking. I'm half in the bag. You know—when you drink so much that you have to close one eye to get the shot down? It was one of those nights. You know how sometimes when you drink you get hungry? Well,

I stopped by Kentucky Fried Chicken and bought a bucket. I went home, turned the television on, put my feet up, ate a leg and fell asleep, or passed out, to be precise. Next thing I know, I'm hearing screams. I jumped up, and there was Liz, screaming at the top of her lungs. It was morning. I was disoriented. I looked on the end-table, and the bucket was empty. On the couch was Gulliver, lying in a bed of chicken bones. It seems he choked."

"You killed the dog?" Frankie couldn't believe it.

"It was an accident. It wasn't murder. It was more like suicide," Tim protested. "But things were never the same after that. Even today, when I pass a fast-food chicken joint, I think of that mutt. Can't help it."

"You're a sensitive man, Tim."

Tim nodded.

"I'm afraid to ask about wife number two."

"Totally not my fault," Tim proclaimed. "I took her boating on Long Island Sound. I had a friend's motorboat. Sweet. We were having a great time. I fixed a picnic basket, a cooler with margaritas, Bloody Mary's, a bottle of Proseco."

"Any food?" Frankie asked.

"I was drinking like it was Saint Patty's day." Tim continued. "Fay was having a great time, too. She was lying in back of the boat, taking in the sun. Anyway, after a few hours, I headed toward the dock. As I got closer, I saw police cars, ambulances, Coast Guard, and EMT wagons on the dock. I turned to ask her what that was all about—and she wasn't there. I kind of did a double take. I mean, it wasn't a big boat, so where could she be? I pulled into the slip, and I was put into handcuffs. I was drunk but sobered up quickly. 'My wife, my wife is gone,' I said. 'What's going on?' I was marched over to an EMT wagon, and there was Fay, wrapped in blankets.

She was shivering, drenched, absolutely water-logged. I'll never forget her eyes, daggers pointed at me. Very similar to the way Liz looked at me, as I think about it now. Seems I hit a wake at some point, and she went off the back. I had no idea. She was in the water for an hour, maybe more, before she was spotted by a fisherman, who alerted the Coast Guard. They thought I did it on purpose, but I had no idea."

"Two hours? You had no idea?"

"Do you know how loud a twin 300 Mercury motor is? I had no idea she'd gone off the back. I was driving the boat. I had my eyes on the road. Anyway, finally she explained to the police that she didn't think I did it on purpose. She didn't press charges, but things were never the same after that. No good deed goes unpunished."

"You, my friend, are a piece of work."

"Do you think they'll come to my wake?" Tim wondered.

"They might, if only to make sure you're dead."

＊　＊　＊

As they drove back to Westchester, Timmy dozed off. Before he did, he asked one more question. "Hey, does Doc look right to you?"

Frankie considered the question. "Why? What do you mean?"

"I don't know. Probably nothing. I just . . . I don't know. Probably nothing."

Frankie thought about the question. He understood what Tim meant. He'd noticed subtle changes in Cardio as well but chalked it up to his imagination. Something always came up, preventing him from inquiring further.

While Tim slept, Frankie thought about the old days with Eddie and his other friend Sal Lucci, his erstwhile manager during his brief stint in showbusiness. The neighborhood, the changes, his life, his old friends, his new friends. It was literally a lifetime ago. His mind came back to how to accomplish the death and disposition of Timmy Collins. He felt certain that he'd have a new identity in a week. The idea of a wake seemed crucial. People on both sides had to see and believe Timmy Collins had died of a heart attack—which was not so hard to believe, given the stress he was under. He remembered Timmy's passing remark about not being able to lie still for any length of time. That was a problem that had to be dealt with. A breathing body would be an issue as well. Frankie thought about a plaster cast of some kind or a mannequin, but those ideas were problematic should someone touch the corpse inadvertently or inadvertently on purpose. Texture was important.

The wake of Timmy Collins would attract mobsters and federal agents, who would attend just to make sure. The local press would be on hand. Usually relegated to covering charity bocce ball tournaments or the opening of an ice rink, this would be a welcome departure for the small-town press corps. Add to that the national coverage that the shooting and subsequent raid received, he was sure the funeral would be well covered. He had to figure something out—and quick. He knew Timmy's days were numbered.

✳

Chapter XIX

Back at the funeral home, Frankie loosened his tie and relaxed on his office couch. Cardio was right about the need to think this through. He broke everything down into different sections. He had taken care of the first obstacle, a new identity. Now he had to think about a way to have everyone believe Timmy was dead. A closed casket or urn would be suspicious. They would have to see him, up close and personal, with their own eyes. It was a challenge.

A phone call came in from the public administrator, Mr. Gregorio. He was on a first-name basis with Frankie. "I want to thank you," he said, "for taking care of Colonel Taffy."

"It was my honor," Frankie replied. "He deserved more than that, but it was the least I could do."

"I know I can always count on you, Frankie. You never let me down. I've got another case pending. Poor soul was found dead at a bus stop just before Christmas. Died of hypothermia. No identification, just a small valise. Been in deep freeze in the morgue since then. I'm trying to track down family, but, if I can't, I may call upon you again. Not a vet, though. We will probably cremate. Can I count on you?"

Frankie did not answer right away. Something clicked in his brain. He considered how the implications of the request could possibly help with his dilemma.

"Frankie. Frankie, are you there?"

"Yes, I'm here, Mr. G. Yes, yes—of course, I'll help." He put the phone down and smiled. A solution had just revealed itself. He picked up the phone and called Cardio and then Timmy. "Meet me in Paradise."

※

Chapter XX

Cardio was waiting at the bar with Johnny and Nino Paradise. Nino was droning on about the clinic and all the treatments available to deal with any malady. Weight loss, sleep apnea, sexual disfunction—all dealt with by cleanses and transfusions of ozone gas. Cardio pretended interest as he popped three painkillers down his throat. He noted that it was one more than he needed yesterday.

At the restaurant, the crew was huddled around the table. Marco began bringing food from the kitchen. "Wait," Johnny said. He walked to the jukebox. He took nothing for granted. He hoped any federal agents who might be listening enjoyed "New York, New York." He pressed D-109.

Frankie filled Cardio and Johnny in on the details of their visit to Mulberry Street. "He'll have a new identity. Without that, we were just spinning our wheels."

"You should have been there, Cardio," Timmy said. "This Eddie guy was the real deal. Right out of the movies."

"More importantly," Cardio asked, "how are you holding up?"

"Me? I'm okay, I guess. I'm not sleeping too well. Cars stop in front of my office every half hour during the night. They stop for a minute and then drive away. Tracy keeps the phone off the hook. Crank calls at all hours. She's a wreck."

"Are you taking the meds?" Cardio asked.

"Yes," he said, looking away.

"So, now what? Does he just skip town?" Johnny asked. Nino was sitting at the bar cracking chestnuts and sharing them with his uncle.

Cardio understood that wouldn't work. "It's not as simple as getting him a new identity. The old identity has to die," he said. "In this case, even more than die—he has to be seen as dead."

"Exactly," Frankie said, "and I just came up with an idea: a body double."

This got everyone's attention, and they moved in closer. Frankie explained, "I got a call from the public administrator. He needs me to take care of the remains of an indigent, an unclaimed body; no family, no friends, no history. He should call me any day."

The men listened. "Okay, I get it. But how do you propose to make that body *that* body?" Johnny said, pointing to Timmy, who was running a comb through his hair while staring in the mirror behind the bar. Timmy turned around, too.

"Yeah, how you gonna do that?"

Frankie was quiet for a moment. "I may know a guy."

"I'll bet you do," Timmy said. "Cardio, you should have been there. This Eddie guy, right out of the movies."

"Assuming you get this body from the county. How do you turn it into him?" Johnny asked.

"We need to visit Chef Gagliardo, also know as, 'The Fixer.' I hope he's still alive."

Frankie explained that there was an embalmer who was a specialist in reconstruction. Embalming was defined as an art and a science. "There are many people," he explained, "who can be taught to raise an artery and inject formaldehyde. But artists are few and far between." Chef Gagliardo was among that chosen few. "Any funeral director who has a difficult case—a head beaten with a baseball bat, a few bullet holes in the face—has called The Chef. He considered it a personal failure if they didn't keep the casket open."

Timmy was confused. "Why did they call him 'The Chef'?"

"He loved to cook, too."

❋

Chapter XXI

Early the next morning, Frankie picked Timmy up and drove to Arthur Avenue in the Bronx. It, too, had been an Italian neighborhood, but what the Chinese did to Little Italy in Manhattan, Mexicans did to Arthur Avenue. Still, there were remnants of the once-famous Italian enclave. Outposts, Italian restaurants, and pasticcericas still brought steady commerce from neighboring Westchester, as they, too, fought the good fight to stay alive in the ever-changing demographic. He stopped by a brownstone, one of many along the street. The sign on the door, dangling from one screw, read "Gagliardo Funeral Home." The wood sign was warped and the colors faded. The small, unassuming structure was much different from Frankie's funeral home. Frankie explained that, around the turn of the century, wakes would be held in people's homes or apartments. Later, funeral homes evolved into storefronts, and from storefronts into the large, multi-chapel funeral homes.

They walked up two steps. A burlap bag wrapped around a fig tree was sitting hunched over on a small patch of grass. Frankie rang the doorbell. In a moment, they heard some shuffling behind the door. Then the peephole slid open. "Who's there?"

"Mr. Gagliardo, it's Frankie Grace."

There was silence for a moment. Then, they heard, "Frankie, Frankie Grace." The man repeated, "Frankie?" The peephole slid shut. There were more rustling noises, and then a series of locks clanged and clicked, and finally the door opened.

A stepstool was leaning against the wall. Gagliardo was wearing a white Guinnea T-shirt tucked into white boxer shorts, black silk knee socks, and sandals. Bifocals hung around his neck. He was pasty white, with a lazy eye that was off in another direction.

"Frankie, Jesus. Frankie Grace, you son of a gun. Is that you? I thought you were dead!" He held out his arms and embraced Frankie. "Come in, come in."

He looked at Timmy with one eye until Frankie assured him, "He's okay. He's with me."

The Chef grabbed a cane and limped down a narrow hallway dimly lit by wall-sconces illuminating cherubs' faces. His club foot dragged along a plastic runner. They followed him down the hall. which led to a small kitchen. There was a parlor off the hallway with a faded-velvet Queen Anne couch. It, too, was covered in plastic. Stained glass windows tinted the sunlight, bathing the parlor in blue and burgundy tones. The colors clung to floating dust particles. The air was musty and stale. Folding chairs were stacked against the wall. Stations of the Cross hung at regular intervals against gold-leaf raised paisley wallpaper. A casket bier and kneeling rail with torchiere lamps were at one end of the room. A miniature replica of Jesus on the cross was suspended from the ceiling, eerily swaying ever so slightly above the casket bier.

In the kitchen behind the parlor, Frankie sat at a Formica-top table. Cabinets lined the wall. Something was simmering in a large cast-iron pot on a four-burner stove; a long wooden spoon lay alongside it. "Let me look at you," The Chef said. "Jesus, I thought I heard you were dead. Must have been somebody else."

"Rumors," Frankie said. "This is my friend Tim."

Timmy reached out to shake hands. "Sit," Gagliardo said. He walked to a cabinet and took out a bottle of Strega and three glasses formerly used for grape jelly. "It's been years," he said. He poured the yellow liquid. "A toast to the old days." He downed the drink in one gulp.

Frankie did the same. "To the old days."

Timmy gagged. Strega was new to him at eight in the morning.

"How's business?" Frankie asked.

"Dead," The Chef answered. "I gave up the business registration years ago. Haven't had a wake here in years. The whole neighborhood is shot. The Spanish place does all the work. This place is a shrine now. When I close my eyes, I'll be laid out here. Then my kids can sell the building to the Albanians. They buy everything that's for sale. They even buy things that are not for sale."

Gagliardo opened a folding chair and sat. His feet were inches off the floor. He poured another round. "Your old man," he reminisced, "I'll never forget him. He was a pain in the ass but a stand-up guy. I remember 1952. You weren't born. I'd just met your old man. We worked together on the Russo hit." He turned to explain to Tim, "Four bullets in the head." He tapped Timmy's forehead four times for emphasis. "Took us hours to restore him. But they kept his casket open. That's saying something. His mother was so happy."

Frankie explained, "I told you, Tim. Mr. Gagliardo is not just an embalmer, he's an artist. The most difficult cases a funeral director has, you call The Fixer. I drink to you. What are you, ninety?"

"Ninety-one," The Chef answered. "Been doing this for seventy years. I filled more holes than Con Edison." He took some aluminum foil off a dish on the table. "*Pinole* cookies," he said pushing the dish toward Timmy.

Frankie laughed and tossed another down. Timmy followed and coughed. "You're in great shape," Frankie noted.

"I'll say," Timmy agreed. "What do you attribute it to?" The Chef poured another round of Strega.

"I have a few drinks every morning and smoke these." He reached for a pack of DiNapoli Italian stogies on the shelf. "Keeps the blood moving and the pecker working. That's important."

The Chef jumped off his chair and walked to the stove. He reached for the wooden spoon, stood on his toes, and stirred the contents of the pot. He brought a sample to his lips. "*Delicioso!*"

Timmy looked around the kitchen. It was a museum of the macabre. There were framed newspaper articles of murders and mob hits hanging on the wall.

Gagliardo noticed him staring. "You see that one? Little Sonny Boy Morano. They put a gun in his mouth and blew his brains out. When I finished my work, you know what his mother said?"

Timmy shook his head.

"'Keep the casket open.' You know the best thing you can tell me? 'Keep the casket open.' That's music to my ears." More Strega.

Timmy walked around the room, examining each article and listening to the story that came with it.

Gagliardo took out a large scrapbook. It was a photo history of every mob hit in the last sixty years. There were thank-you notes from survivors for making it possible to say goodbye. There were before-and-after Polaroid pictures of bullet-ridden bodies.

Tim flipped through the pages in bug-eyed amazement.

"You see," The Chef explained, "when you get whacked in the face, the boys are sending a message. Your family will never see you again, not even in a casket. I fooled a few wise guys in my days. Wouldn't you say, Frankie?"

Frankie lifted his glass. "Yeah, you disappointed a few."

"Remember the Zambino incident?" The Chef asked.

"I sure do," Frankie said.

Tim shrugged his shoulders as Frankie explained. "The Chef did such a good job on Bobby 'Big Head' Zambino, the guy who'd ordered the hit was not happy. During the night, someone broke into the funeral home."

The Chef continued the story. "When I came down the next morning and flipped on the lights, Bobby had no head. A precision cut, real professional. I was impressed." He flipped through the scrapbook. "Here," he said pointing to a *Daily News* article, 'Wise-guy Loses His Head.' "Hours of work out the window," The Chef lamented. "The head was never found. It might still be somewhere in this building, for all I know."

Tim shifted in his chair.

"Anyway, after that, they called him 'Bobby the Neck.'" The Chef pointed with pride to the Polaroid pictures of the headless corpse he had Scotch-taped alongside the article. "You can't win them all." Tim felt gastric juices making their way up his esophagus. He swallowed hard.

Tim turned the page in the scrapbook. "Luciano?" he said in amazement.

The Chef nodded, explaining, "January 1962, I was sitting in my chair. The doorbell rang. It was Tony 'Three Finger' Dundee, our local neighborhood boss. "Chef," he said, "we need your help. In two hours, I was at Idlewild with nothing but my instruments and an overnight bag. There's a plane waiting. Next stop—Naples, Italy. Lucky had had a fatal heart attack in an airport in Naples a few days earlier. He was allowed to be buried back in America, although he had been deported as part of a deal that released him from prison. You know, he helped us beat the Germans with his union connections in Italy. So, the feds let him out of prison but deported him. Anyway, it took weeks to get him back. He looked like he'd died yesterday when he arrived back home."

Timmy was amazed at the wall of honor. For The Chef, the greatest mob hits were not a CD by Jerry Vale. Every rubout from Uale, Galante, Gallo, Castellano. Timmy felt a sudden chill. If Frankie's plan failed, the services of this man, sitting in his underwear, drinking Strega and puffing on a cigar that produced an inordinate amount of smoke and stench, may be needed. The thought caused him to shudder.

"So, why are you here, Frankie?"

Frankie downed the drink and poured another. He walked up to Timmy. "You see this face, Chef? I need another one just like it. Can you help?"

A little smile came across The Chef's face. It was good to be needed. He took Timmy's face in his hands, turning it one way and then the other. "Why this face? Don't you want me to improve it?"

"Just like it is, Chef." Frankie said.

The Chef nodded. "Follow me."

The three men walked down basement steps to the preparation room. The funeral home had not been active in many years. Metal cabinets lined the room. Peeling labels warned that they housed hazardous chemicals. Scalpels, forceps, curved needles, sutures, and other tools of the trade were sitting, shining, on a metal tray alongside a porcelain embalming table. It had an antique, ghoulish feel to it. The air was stagnant. The Chef cracked a door that led to a ramp and a backyard. Cold air rushed in. He pointed to a small patch of earth fenced in. "Frankie, come back in the summer. I'll give you some eggplant and zucchini. I grow the best."

The Chef was an optimist, Frankie noted. The thought of eating anything from this garden gave Timmy more chills.

"You," The Chef ordered, tapping the embalming table. "Take off your shirt and that mop off your head, and sit up here." The Chef was observant for ninety-one. Timmy had to give him that much. Tim removed his jacket and shirt and, reluctantly, his hairpiece. He handed it to Frankie, who accepted it with two fingers. He placed it on the counter.

"Do you have another one of these?" Frankie asked as a thought came to him.

"There's not a self-respecting bald man who only has one toupee. I happen to have five." He sat on the embalming table as The Chef went about taking materials out of cabinets.

The Chef donned a white apron and put a barber's cape over Timmy, leaving his head exposed. He was trance-like as he limped around the room. The experience of seventy years propelled him. With a pair of scissors in his hand, he approached Timmy, whose eyes widened. "Relax," The Chef said. "I've never killed anyone. They were already dead when they got here." He laughed out loud, and Frankie did, too. He began to trim Timmy's eyebrows and sideburns, catching the hair in a tissue. "You'll need these," he said, as he placed the tissue into a baggie. Frankie nodded.

The Chef rubbed Vaseline on Timmy's eyebrows and into the remaining remnants of hair above his sideburns. On the counter, he mixed an amalgam of silicone with other ingredients, as if following an ancient recipe. "Just keep your mouth shut, and breathe through here," he said, tapping Timmy's nose. "It's big enough. You should get plenty of air."

Frankie sat back in amazement, watching a master at work, admiring his dexterity and skill. It must have been this way for students of DaVinci or Michelangelo. The Chef applied the mixture to Tim's face with a small spatula. He spread it meticulously across his cheekbones, nose, and chin. In minutes, Timmy's head was covered. And as he watched, Frankie was also deep in thought about the whole plan. For some reason that he wasn't aware of, he said, "His hands, Chef. Can we do the hands?"

The Chef nodded and repeated the procedure on Timmy's hands.

"This should set in no time," The Chef said. "When you cosmeticize, use an air-brush. I don't have to tell *you*, I guess." The Chef may have wondered why the mask was needed but never asked. Frankie could count on that. The Chef was old-school, a man who had seen a lot and could be trusted. He never asked any questions. Frankie had made a request, and that was all he needed to know.

He limped up the stairs and came down with a bottle of wine and *soperssata*. "I made this," he said, as he cut through the dried sausage with a scalpel. "I warn you. It's hot." The two men ate and drank, waiting for the amalgamate to dry. Timmy sat still, listening to old stories about different funerals and mob shootings. The Chef had a photographic memory.

"You should write a book," Frankie suggested.

The Chef laughed. "As long as I change the names to protect the guilty."

When the wine was finished, The Chef gently ran his finger along Timmy's temple. He was satisfied with the result. From a cabinet, he pulled out a styrofoam head and set it down on the table. He walked back to Timmy. "Just relax," he said. "You will feel a little pull on your skin. Don't fight it. Relax."

The Chef put his fingers on the back of Timmy's neck and pulled as gently and easy as removing a Halloween mask. He put the finished product over the styrofoam head. Then he peeled the rubber amalgam off Tim's hands as easily as taking off a glove. "Keep your eyes closed," he said. He poured witch hazel on a washcloth and put it in Timmy's hands. "Wipe your face with this."

Timmy ran the cloth over his face, slowly opening his eyes. When he did, he was staring at himself, as The Chef was holding the replica in front of his eyes. "Amazing," Timmy said. It was a double.

"Yeah," The Chef said. "Now, there are two *faccia brutto*!"

"Amazing," he said again. "Is there any more wine?"

The Chef laughed. "You guys staying for lunch? I made tripe."

"What's tripe?" Timmy asked.

The Chef looked at Frankie. "Irish?" he asked.

Frankie nodded. "I'll tell you after you eat it," he said to Tim.

☀

Chapter XXII

Tracy Collins thought it wise to have her slip-and-fall attorney and cousin accompany her to an interview with Reno Amore. Bernie explained to her that this was not his field of expertise. Doing due diligence, he Googled Reno Amore and was already intimidated by the bio and numerous news articles. He tried to dissuade her, suggesting a criminal lawyer might be more helpful, but she insisted. Besides, the price was right. Bernie was family.

"What can go wrong?" she asked. "I haven't done anything wrong. We answer a few questions, and we leave."

In the same field office where her husband had sat a week earlier, Reno Amore introduced himself. Bernie wondered if Amore felt the moisture that formed in his palm as he shook hands. His hand felt like a wet fish being squeezed by Captain Ahab.

"I, I'm Bernie, Bernard, Bernard Schwartz," he said wondering why he'd said his name three times. "And you know Tracy Collins. I, I'm here with her. I mean, we came together. I mean . . ."

"He's my lawyer," Tracy jumped in.

"Please sit. Thank you for coming," Amore said.

The three sat around the table. "May I ask what this is about?" Bernie asked.

"Well, actually it's a courtesy. I assume you're aware of the criminal indictment we have on Mr. Collins. It amounts to dozens of counts, from mail fraud, money laundering, gambling, fraud, wire fraud."

Bernie's eyebrows twitched as he stared at Tracy. "Well, I wasn't actually aware of that, but I can assure you that Tracy—Mrs. Collins—has nothing to do with any criminal or nefarious activities."

Amore opened a file. "Well, I'd *like* to believe that," he said as he went through the file. "But it seems there is a matter of tax fraud and mortgage fraud to begin with."

"I don't know what you're talking about," Tracy said. "I don't know what he's talking about," she said to her cousin." Bernard patted her arm.

"As she said, she doesn't have any knowledge of any criminal activity."

Amore slid papers across the table. Bernard picked them up and looked through them. "These are tax returns?"

"Yes," Amore said, "tax returns," he added. "And," he said, sliding more documents across the table, "these are mortgage documents."

"What's your point?" Tracy asked.

"They're fraudulent," Amore said. "All fraudulent tax returns and bank loans, and your name is on all of them."

Bernard took antacid tablets from his pocket and reached for a pitcher of water. He poured it into a cup, spilling most on the table. He whispered in Tracy's ear, "Tracy, is everything gone? All his investments?" She nodded "Yes." He turned to Amore. "My cousin—my client—is unaware . . ."

"I know nothing about any of my husband's business. He puts papers in front of me and tells me to sign, so I sign. I trusted him. I had no reason to doubt or question him."

Amore spoke in soothing tones. "Unfortunately, as your cousin—I mean, attorney—will tell you, your signature makes you liable for the fraud. Ignorance of what you signed is not a defense. Your attorney can confirm that."

"That's impossible," Tracy cut in.

Bernard reached out to touch her arm. "What exactly are you looking for from Mrs. Collins?" he asked.

❋　❋　❋

In the elevator, Bernard asked, "Tracy, as far as you know, are all Tim's businesses involved in this? Are you sure?"

"That's what I'm hearing. Why?"

"*Oy vey,*" he answered.

❋

Chapter XXIII

Tim's cell phone woke him during the ride back from the city. Frankie heard Tracy yelling.

"You son of a bitch," she screamed. Among a myriad of Yiddish words and phrases—the tone of which suggested a negative connotation—she managed to tell Tim of her meeting with Mr. Amore.

Timmy was distraught at the news. He put the phone away. "Man," he said, "I made a mess of things. I got Tracy in the crosshairs. She's frazzled. They can squeeze her. As my wife, she wasn't able to testify against me. Even though we're still married, that means nothing anymore. Her name is on all the papers I faked."

"He'll play her, for sure," Frankie agreed.

"And you guys are about to walk the plank for me with this harebrained plan. Maybe, I should . . . ."

"Should what?" Frankie asked.

"If I had any guts, I'd jump off a bridge and save everyone a lot of trouble."

"You're talking stupid," Frankie said. "Life sucks as it is. It always throws you a curve. You're going along, things are fine. Like the doc said, you think you got the world by the balls—and then the bottom falls out. It's always something. Maybe you dying is the only way to derail this Amore guy. You are his prize. If you're dead, there's no prize."

Tim just nodded. "I hope you're right."

It was time for another planning session. It was time for Frankie to explain just how to accomplish this very dubious plan. He wasn't sure, either, and spent the time sitting in traffic on the Cross Bronx Expressway, trying to figure it out.

※

Chapter XXIV

Johnny met them in the parking lot. "I'm worried about you guys," Johnny said. "Cardio's been here an hour already. He's in the head. He's been drinking, too. Not like him. He can't seem to hold his liquor."

"Come on," Frankie objected. "Cardio's no slouch."

"No, I mean it literally," Johnny explained. "He dropped two drinks and nearly choked on an olive. He's as nervous as all of us, I guess. Come in." Frankie took the box out of his car and waked into the restaurant. There were embraces all around as they gathered at the table.

"Are you guys okay?" Cardio asked. This was not an ordinary gathering of the Romeo Club. Drinks weren't making them jolly. The concern on their face was palatable. They were edgy, worn, frazzled.

"We're fine. What about you?" Frankie asked.

"Just worried. I'm watching the news. The feds are on the march," Cardio observed.

They sat around the table. Frankie put the box on the bar. Johnny punched some numbers into the jukebox. Sinatra started singing "That's Life." "So, where are we in this thing?" he asked.

"Yeah, how is this going to work?" Cardio asked.

Nino brought food to the table. Then he went to the bar for wine. He saw the box on the counter and looked in it. *"Ah! Ah!"* he screamed at the sight of the head.

Johnny jumped up. "What is it, *nipote*?" The blood had drained from Nino's face. "Did you see a mouse?" his uncle asked.

Frankie laughed as he took the box to the table. He pointed to Timmy. "I guess the only thing scarier than that face is two of them." He tilted the box so all could see The Chef's creation. Then he passed it around.

"Very impressive," Cardio said.

"I'll say," Johnny agreed.

"So, here it is. This is key. Jump in anytime if you foresee any problems or have suggestions. Now is the time," Frankie said.

Johnny laughed. *"Foresee any problems?* We are faking the death of someone wanted by three federal agencies and just as many mobs. What problems can you possibly see?"

"That's why we have to be perfect. Here's what I'm thinking," Frankie said. "We are certain that Timmy will have a new identity in a few days. I guarantee it. To go along with the new identity, now we have this. Here's what I'm thinking: Hopefully, any day now, I get that call from the public administrator. He will ask me to have the unclaimed body cremated. When I get John Doe, I use that mask to make it look like Timmy and have a wake. I had been thinking of using a mannequin, but this makes more sense. It will be more lifelike—should someone touch the body."

"I don't want to be cremated," Timmy said as an aside.

"Shut up, idiot," Frankie answered.

But Tim continued, "And if I were cremated, I would think of something along the lines of a Viking funeral. Something with a bit more pizzazz. You know, they put the body on a boat and set it on fire."

"I had a cousin," Johnny joined in. "He had a Viking funeral, Italian style. They stuffed him in his trunk, set the car on fire, and rolled it off Pier 6 off the West Side Highway."

Everyone digested that anecdote.

"Back up," Cardio said, hoping to change the subject. "It isn't as easy as putting a mask on another body. There will be people following every step of the way, from the place of death, to the funeral home, to the crematory."

"I want a funeral mass, too," Timmy said.

"Shut up, idiot." It was Johnny this time.

"Here's what I'm thinking, just for argument's sake. He's been sleeping in his office. When I get the John Doe, I will bring him to Timmy's office. I'll find a way to discover his body. I'll say he didn't answer the phone, and I went over. I will stage the body, cover it with a blanket, and then follow procedure."

Cardio knew the drill from that point. "The police will come and call the medical examiner. The coroner may decide to do an autopsy and send the meat wagon. We're screwed if that happens."

Johnny wondered, "Why do you have to call the cops?"

"An unattended death has to be called in to the police," Cardio explained, "unless you are under hospice care."

"That's why you will have to convince the coroner it's a normal death. Nothing suspicious. He was under your care for years. You know the routine," Frankie said.

"Yes," Cardio said. "But, if for some reason, the coroner *does* decide to claim the body for autopsy, we are dead."

"And what happens when the police come to the office and see John Doe and not Timmy, duh?" Johnny asked.

"Look," Frankie said, "I know every cop in this town. I never met one who wants to be in a room with a dead body, especially one that will, no doubt, be in a state of decomposition."

"That might be a problem," Cardio said. "Why would the body be decomposed so quickly? The officer may wonder."

Frankie digested the observation. "Good point," he said. "It could work both ways, as well. The cop might not want to get close, and, with my assurance that I know who it is under the blanket, he will be happy to stand in the hallway until the coroner gives clearance. I'll have to make sure of that or think of some reason why he decomposed so fast."

"I guess that's where I come in," Cardio said.

"Exactly. I tell the police I've called his doctor. You come and make the official pronouncement of death and report it to the coroner."

"It gets tricky there," Cardio said. He placed his glasses on the table and rubbed his temples. "Again, if the coroner wants to do an autopsy, he can call for the body. He can override me."

"Can't we cite a religious objection to an autopsy? My wife is Jewish," Tim said.

"And you're a pagan," Frankie answered.

"If the coroner does order an autopsy, we're screwed. Game over," Johnny rightly observed.

Frankie nodded. He pointed to Cardio. "That's why you have to convince him that he died from a long-standing heart condition. You are his longtime physician. Hopefully, they will be busy and won't want to add another body to the list. They should be fine with you signing his death certificate. And, I guess I should ask: *Are* you willing to sign his death certificate? You know what it means if we get caught. You will lose your license. Maybe prison."

"There are many moving parts," Nino observed.

Johnny brought more food to the table. "I'm confused. You make one body look like Timmy. What happens to the Doe body?"

"He'll be cremated looking like Timmy," Frankie acknowledged.

"You'll have one body, but two death certificates," Cardio pointed out.

Timmy seemed absent from the planning session. He was writing on cocktail napkins. "What are you doing?" Cardio finally asked.

"Bullet points . . . for my eulogy," he answered.

Everyone shook their heads in disbelief.

Johnny tried to summarize. "So, you have a Doe body, which you dress up with this thing," he said, pointing to the box. "Then you throw a wake so everyone can see him in the casket and be satisfied that he's dead. Will that be it? Will they be satisfied?"

"I want a funeral mass," Timmy said. "They'll think something is fishy if I don't have a funeral mass."

"Yeah—you being a good Catholic and all," Frankie said.

"I want a mass," he insisted.

"May not be a bad idea," Johnny said. "It will look better."

There was quiet around the table as they ate and drank.

Cardio reached for some macaroni that had been brought to the table. "You are going to have two death certificates. You will need to produce two bodies," he said again.

"Good point. Let's think," Frankie said. "We must be missing something."

"It sounds like a simple plan," Nino offered. "You need only fool the police, the medical examiner, the FBI, the mafia, and the Chinese and Albanian warlords. Am I leaving anyone out?"

"Yes," Frankie said. "I have to fool the attendant at the crematory." He explained that, if he intended to have the John Doe body cremated looking like Timmy, at some point, he'd have to bring another body to be cremated. "There are two death certificates that need to be accounted for. The casket will have to have some weight to it, and—more importantly—the crematory attendant will have to see bone remnants when he opens the retort door. There will have to be skeletal remains in the cremation retort after the process is finished. Those bones are ultimately processed into what we call ashes."

"So, we need weight and bones?" Cardio asked.

"Yes."

"I may be able to help with that," Cardio offered.

Frankie sat back. "Good enough for me," he said. He soaked the heel of Italian bread in his glass of wine. "I think we have thought about almost everything."

"What about a funeral luncheon?" Timmy asked. "There are going to be a lot of people."

"I guess we should do something here—a buffet, maybe," Johnny offered.

"Buffet!" The word stung Timmy as much as the word "cremation." "I can't do a buffet. Do you want people to think I'm cheap? Has to be a sit-down luncheon." He stopped writing. "I'm exhausted. So much to say in so little time. I mean, how do you put a man's life into a few paragraphs. How do you capture the essence of me? I never died before. I don't know what life after my death looks like. You think this is easy for me? No one wants to be the guest of honor at the funeral luncheon. It will be the first party I ever missed. I only get one chance to die, and I want to do it right."

"Is that all you can think about?" Cardio asked.

Tim put his pen down. "I'm sorry, guys. The truth is . . . I guess I have writer's block. I'm thinking and thinking and can't come up with anything nice to say about me. I'm a fraud, a total fraud. I've ruined my life. I've spent half my money on wine, women, and song—and the rest I've wasted. I've put you guys behind the eight-ball, got my wife in the crosshairs, left a legacy of debt, and stole from people who trusted me. I don't deserve anything you guys are doing for me. I should just face the music with the feds."

"Listen to me, you mook." Johnny was adamant. "Do you understand what these guys are doing for you? If it doesn't work, they will be in a jail cell next to you. You gotta get ahold of yourself."

"I know, I know. I'm grateful. You gotta know, if nothing else, I don't deserve friends like you."

"Listen," Frankie said, "timing is key. Hopefully, I'll get this call from the public administrator. When I do, we will have to move quickly. Tim, you will have to crash in my office for a few days. Get some clothes and essentials. Don't make it look obvious. Tracy won't be suspicious. She'll think you're preparing to move out, which is what she wants. And bring me one of those," he said, pointing to his head. "And a jogging suit or loungewear of some kind."

"Does he look like he jogs?" Cardio asked.

Everyone nodded. "What then? Where do I go after I die? Do I just get on a train and disappear?"

"I offered. You can come home with me," Nino said. Johnny, Cardio, and Frankie chewed on the idea, along with peppers, olive-oil-laced bread, stuffed artichokes, and a bottle of Amarone.

❋

Chapter XXV

Frankie and Timmy parked on Broom Street and began walking down Mulberry Street. As they passed a newsstand, Frankie stopped short, his eyes focused on the image on the front page of the *New York Post*. The jacket caught his eye. It was bright blue, embroidered with an elaborate floral design. The man wearing it was accompanied by two men holding his arms. Eddie Fontana had been arrested overnight. Frankie bought the paper and began reading on the sidewalk. The headline read, "FBI orders take-out from Ciao Mein."

He read aloud, "In what appears to be the aftermath of a sweeping arrest made last week, don Eddie Fontana, acting head of the Ballsziti crime family, was arrested late yesterday in his headquarters at Ciao Mein Restaurant. He will be arraigned today on a 14-count federal indictment that includes loansharking, gambling, and money laundering."

"Jesus," Timmy said. "I'm screwed. Maybe it's a sign. Let's call the whole thing off."

Frankie stared at the front page and looked at the photograph of his friend being led from the restaurant. Eddie did not hide from the camera. Instead, he had a shit-ass grin. He was quoted in the caption below the photo, "Try the Peking Duck. It's the best in the city." Those were not the only words Fontana uttered as he was led away in handcuffs. Reporters said they were unintelligible. Frankie threw the paper in the trash.

"Let me think, let me think," he said. He paced up and down, calling Eddie's name out loud.

"What do we do now?" Timmy asked.

Instinct took over. "Come on," Frankie said. They continued walking down Mulberry to the restaurant. The two Asian men they'd met on their first trip to see Eddie were standing outside the restaurant. Frankie nodded politely, and one of them acknowledged him. After a moment, he motioned Frankie inside. The other man stopped Timmy. Frankie followed and watched the man as he removed the candle from the base of the Buddha. Then, he reverently removed the Buddha from its alcove. He tapped on the back wall. A trap door opened. He reached in, pulled out a leather pouch from the wall, and handed it to Frankie. Frankie took the pouch. "Thank you," he said. The man nodded. Frankie's hands were trembling; his heart was pounding against his chest. He was glad he'd followed his instincts. He knew his friend Eddie would not disappoint him. He stuffed the package under his arm and took deep breaths before walking back out onto the sidewalk.

He adjusted his eyes to the daylight. "Let's go," he said to Timmy.

"What happened?" Timmy asked.

"Quiet—just keep walking." The two men hurried back to the car.

"What do you think is in it?" Timmy asked, looking at the pouch.

"I'm afraid to look," Frankie said. Frankie's heart was still pounding. Sweat was beading on his brow, and his hands were shaking.

"I'm getting too old for this. Let's get back to Paradise and open it there. Call, and tell Johnny we are on our way."

*   *   *

An FBI agent relaxing in the FedEx truck also wondered what was in the pouch. He picked up the phone.

*

Chapter XXVI

*B*ack at the restaurant, the crew gathered around the table. Frankie was still shaking. He put the portfolio on the table. "You won't believe this," he said. "We got downtown, and I saw that my friend Eddie had been arrested. *Jesus,* I thought, *that's it. It's over.*" Johnny placed a finger over his lips, motioning all to keep quiet. He walked to the jukebox; he played #C-15, "Big Bad Leroy Brown." He reached behind the jukebox and raised the volume.

"You should have met this guy, Cardio. He was the real deal," Timmy asserted. "And he goes and gets pinched."

"I could have told you that," Johnny said, "It's on the local news."

Frankie explained, "Anyway, I'm thinking and thinking. I know Eddie so well. I know he'd find a way. So, we walk down to the restaurant, just hoping against hope—and *bingo*! One of his cronies takes me inside. Eddie made contingency plans for just this kind of thing. He knew I'd still come by even if something unforeseen had happened to him. I know him like a book." He pointed to the pouch. "So, here it is."

"Have you looked in it?" Nino asked.

Frankie and Timmy shook their heads.

Cardio reached over and unzipped the pouch, pulling out a fistful of documents. There was a passport. He opened it up, stared at it, and then stared at Timmy. "Unreal," he said. He passed it around the table. The forgery was masterful.

"You have a new identity. You are now Luciano Greco." He handed the passport to Timmy.

Timmy stared at it for a few seconds, and tears formed in his eyes.

"What's wrong?" Johnny asked.

Tim wiped his eyes. He was choked up. "I always wanted to be Italian. There, I admit it."

✳   ✳   ✳

Eddie Fontana had outdone himself. Tim Collins was now Luciano Greco. There was an Italian birth certificate and accompanying documentation, including an Italian driver's license. Greco had been born in Rome and had a passport issued by the European Union. Tim—AKA Luciano—would be free to travel all over the world, no questions asked. And there was more. Tim reached into the pouch and pulled out a paperback book. *Italian for Idiots.*

Frankie laughed out loud. It was textbook Eddie.

"This calls for a celebration," Cardio said.

"Yes, yes," Timmy agreed. "Nino, a bottle of your best cheap wine. It's on your uncle."

"A toast," Frankie said, "SPQR! The senate and the people of Rome."

The newly minted documents were passed around the table. "I told you this Eddie guy was the real deal," Tim said.

"It's a master forgery," Cardio agreed as he examined the documents.

Food kept coming out of the kitchen. Frankie explained that now it was just a waiting game. The next part of the plan would commence, followed by the wake.

Speech was slurred, laughs were loud, and conversation was unintelligible. "Wait, wait," Cardio said. "How are we going to walk up to his casket, knowing what we know, and not crack up laughing?"

The question sobered everyone. Nino whispered into his uncle's ear. Johnny smiled and nodded. "I'll take care of that," he said. Everyone exchanged glances.

"Good enough for me," Frankie said. As he spoke, his phone vibrated from within his jacket. He answered and walked away from the table, looking for a quiet corner. He was somber when he returned to the table.

"That was the public administrator." He looked at Tim. "You just died. The public administrator couldn't track down any family. Your body double is ready for pickup." The reality of the plan they embarked upon suddenly hit them. The silence caused Frankie to speak. "We don't have to continue," Frankie said. "We can stop now—no harm, no foul."

The remark hung out there in the air as the men thought. Breaking news—complete with the accompanying alarming soundtrack—helped make the decision. News 12 reported that the FBI had an informant embedded in the Albanian cartel who would bring down the entire operation.

"They're squeezing Tim," Johnny said. "The feds plant a story like that to squeeze him. They're spooking the bad guys into making a move on Tim, hoping Tim runs to them for help."

The normally raucous group was subdued.

Johnny, Nino, Cardio, and the soon-to-be-late Timmy Collins exchanged glances. Tim stood up. "Guys, I'm gonna turn myself in and make the deal. I'm putting you all in danger. This is my problem. I can't get you involved."

The conspirators listened to the offer. "Let's vote," Nino suggested.

"It has to be unanimous," Johnny said. "One 'No' vote, and it's off."

Frankie agreed. "Cardio, you're senior man here. You start."

"I say we do it. We save our friend."

Johnny was next. "Agreed."

"Do I get a vote?" Nino asked.

"You get half a vote," Frankie said. "We only just met you."

Nino understood. "I put my half vote in favor."

Now everyone looked to Frankie.

He raised a glass. *"Morte!"* he said. Everyone drank. Frankie looked at his watch. "This will go down tonight. Go get some clothes and necessities. Don't make it look obvious. Tracy will assume you're getting ready to move out. Just a few things, like I said. Remember, you won't see Tracy again. So, do what you have to do before you leave—and don't forget to bring one of those." He pointed to his toupee. "Then go to your office, and call Johnny. He will pick you up at your office and take you to my office. Your car has to be at your office. You'll crash at my place until we make plans to fly you out. Nino can make the arrangements." Frankie's mind was in overdrive. He was talking at warp speed; as thoughts entered his head, they passed his lips. "I'm headed to the medical examiner's office," he said. "All the clearance and paperwork is ready for me. Are we all agreed?"

Again, all nodded.

"Cardio, remember—when I call you to come to pronounce Tim dead, there will be police there. We need to play it straight. No

hugs. Just keep it professional—like we hardly know each other."
Another thought came to Frankie's head. "Give me your watch."

"My watch?" Tim was confused.

"Just give it to me."

Reluctantly, Tim unbuckled the watch. "It was an engagement
present. It's a Patek." He handed it over. Frankie examined it. The
back was inscribed, "Tim, love Tiff."

"Perfect. Who's Tiff?" Frankie asked.

"Tiffany, an old flame. We were engaged," Tim explained. "The
flame died out. I kept the Patek, and she kept the ring." He laughed.
"I got the better of the deal. The diamond was a zirconium."

Frankie hustled out the door. "By the way, Tim," he stopped
to say, "Patek is spelled with a 'k,' not a 'c.'" Tim was left with his
mouth open. Johnny, Nino, and Cardio could not contain their smile.

"A knockoff? That swindler," Tim said.

After a moment, Nino said, "I will make the reservations."

"Nino," Timmy called out. "I don't do well in coach."

❊

Chapter XXVII

Cardio left the restaurant feeling dizzy. The combination of booze and meds was not good. Johnny drove him to his apartment building. "Are you okay, Cardio? Do you want me to come up?" Johnny asked.

"Fine. I'm fine."

"I can come up with you," he offered again.

"I'm fine," he said.

As Cardio walked into the building, Johnny watched and had a feeling that his friend wasn't fine. He wobbled into his building, his body like Jello as he took hold of a rail alongside the walkway.

✳   ✳   ✳

Back at the restaurant, the Thursday-night crowd was settling in. There was not a seat to be had. Nino was busy working the bar, mixing a concoction he billed as a ". . . healthy cocktail . . ." He placed mushrooms and beets in a blender with a combination of juices; he added various spirits, Grenadine, and bitters. Patrons stood at the bar taking selfies with old man Paradise's portrait in the background. Johnny explained to all who asked, who was where when the bullets flew. The story changed every time, embellished just enough to keep the celebrity going. Johnny was reflective. He took a deep breath. "Can you believe this?" he asked his nephew. "If I had known this, I would have taken a few shots at Timmy years ago."

☀

Chapter XXVIII

Frankie pulled his removal van into the loading dock at the coroner's office. He wheeled a stretcher into the staging area and went to the desk. After preliminary pleasantries, he stated his business. The clerk was aware of the reason that Frankie had come and pulled the file that included the death certificate and permission for Frankie to take charge of the body. Frankie was uncharacteristically nervous, not even checking the paperwork he signed. The disgruntled morgue attendant walked him down a row of refrigerated morgue boxes, one indistinguishable from the next. Each held human remains, different lives, different stories, histories, different endings. Kings and peasants share the same cold-room, wrapped unceremoniously in white plastic, useless to contain leakage. A daily grim reminder of his own mortality. *Who wouldn't love this job?* he thought.

The attendant stopped, pulled on a handle, and slid out a stainless-steel tray. A human form in white plastic became visible.

"Here she is," the attendant said. The words resonated as he moved to slide the corpse from the tray onto his stretcher. The arm fell to the side of the body at the moment Frankie realized why the morgue attendant's words stuck with him: "Here, *she* is." To complicate matters, the hand that became visible was black. It seemed that the body double for Tim Collins would be a black woman. "Are you okay?" the attendant asked, sensing Frankie's hesitation.

"Huh? Yes. Yes, I'm okay," he answered. This would be his first transgender funeral.

Frankie concluded that it did not really change the essence of the plan. It was nearly 8 p.m. as he drove back to Inlet Cove. He opened all the windows for fresh air. As the refrigeration wore off, the effects of decomposition became more evident. The odor, like sulfur, the devil's cologne, decaying internal organs. He hoped the odor would be helpful in keeping the responding officer at bay and also thought about how to explain the rapid decomposition.

The moon was full and reflected off the inlet. As he drove, he knew that he could nix the plan at any time. His friends would understand. He rolled the stretcher onto the lift and then down into the preparation room. The odor was nauseating—rotten eggs, a smell that would stay with him long into the night. The worse the odor, the better, in this case. In the embalming room, he got his first good look at the body double for Tim Collins. He moved her onto the embalming table. She was skeletal. The breach of trust gnawed at him. He hesitated before finally proceeding, trying to convince himself of the greater good. He apologized out loud to Jane Doe and then proceeded to tape a pillow to her torso, adding bulk, before dressing her in Tim's jogging suit. Methodically, he placed the rubber mask over her head. Then, he moved the body back onto the stretcher and out into the van. As he drove toward the Collins Agency, he again thought about ending the plan. He could make a U-turn and drive back to the funeral home. As he came to the intersection, he thought one more time. *It isn't too late. Everyone will understand.* Adrenaline took over. Slowly, he made a right turn and headed toward the Collins Agency. There was little traffic on this winter evening. He passed in front of the building, circling the block three times; then he turned into the driveway leading to a small parking lot. Tim's car was in its reserved spot. He backed up to the rear entrance of Tim's office and realized he didn't have a key. He fumbled with his phone and called Tim.

"What's wrong?" Tim asked.

"Nothing, nothing—except I don't have a key to get into your office."

"It's a keypad. Press 7 11."

Frankie approached the door and pressed the numbers. He heard a click, and the door opened. "Okay. Just sit tight. Here we go."

Frankie rolled the stretcher into the darkened space. He was familiar with Tim's office, having visited many times. He wheeled the stretcher adroitly between desks and chairs, past a water dispenser, and into Tim's office. Behind the desk was a swivel chair. Frankie unzipped the pouch on the stretcher and picked up the corpse. She weighed no more than a hundred pounds, from what he could guess. For that he was happy. "Jane," he said, "I'm really sorry about this, but my friend is in trouble. Just think of it as helping to save a life." He set her carefully into the chair. She was light but still frigid and did not fit into the contour of the chair. He decided to lay her on the floor behind the desk, posing her in various positions. He went back to the door to see how it would look when an officer came into the room. He thought it would be better to see more torso, so he moved the body a bit from behind the desk. Then he thought it a would be a good idea to flip the chair to the side as if it had fallen over when the body fell, hands trapped beneath. That would solve the color issue. From the doorway, that looked better. He took the blanket from the stretcher and covered the body. Then he opened a desk lamp and moved it to cast a shadow across the room. The spookier, the better. When he was satisfied, he pulled out his phone. The Inlet Cove Police Department was on speed dial. As he called, he saw the thermostat. He turned it up to ninety.

"Inlet Cove Police, Officer Mallory."

"Hey, Chuck. It's Frankie Grace."

"Hey, Mr. Grace. How are you?"

"I'm fine, Chuck. How's your mom? How is she doing?"

"Ah, it's tough. You know, but she's doing the best she can. Can't thank you enough for the beautiful funeral for my dad."

"Hey, thank you. That means a lot. If you need anything, more thank-you cards—anything at all—you know you can call."

"Yeah, thanks. We are getting around to that now. What can I do for you?"

Frankie took a deep breath and cleared his throat. "Actually," he said, "I have to report a death. I stopped by my friend Timmy Collins' office and found him there."

"Oh, boy. That's too bad. I know Tim, too. Anything unusual?"

"No, not at all. He left lunch early today. Said he had indigestion. We were supposed to meet for dinner, but he never answered the phone."

"Well, he's had his hands full lately, from what I read and hear. This might be the best thing, considering what he had to look forward to."

"Maybe you're right, Chuck. He's been under a lot of stress."

"I can only imagine. Had to weigh on him. Anyway, I'll radio a unit to come by. Let me see. Yeah, I'll send Billy Hopper. He's in the area."

"Hopper?" Frankie asked.

"Yeah. Go easy on him. He's fresh out of the academy, a proby, a little green. This will be his first stiff."

If you think he's green now, Frankie thought. "Thanks, Chuck."

"No problem. Sorry, about your friend, Mr. Grace. I dispatched him. He should be there in five minutes."

"Fine," Frankie said. "I'll call Tim's doctor as well. Give your mom a hug." Frankie wheeled the stretcher back into the van and moved it to a dark corner of the lot. He returned to the office sweating profusely; his insides were trembling. He called Cardio. "It's time," he said. "Come to Tim's office."

In minutes, he saw a red strobe light and walked out to greet officer Hopper.

The baby-faced officer with bright, rosy cheeks approached Frankie. "What do we have here?" he asked with an air of authority.

Frankie introduced himself. "It's Tim Collins," Frankie said. "I was supposed to take him to dinner. When he didn't answer I came over. He's been under a lot of stress. I called his doctor; he's on the way."

Hopper followed Frankie through the darkened office. When they reached Tim's office, Frankie opened the door. The odor hit them in the face. Even in the darkness, Frankie could see the bloom come off the rose as the color drained from the young officer's face. Hopper stared at the human form on the floor behind the desk. His knees seemed to buckle. The lamplight cast a shadow across the wall. The officer took a step forward and then began to gag. Frankie moved to his side and guided him to the restroom off the outer office. From outside, he heard the officer regurgitating—then water running, then more regurgitating, then more water running. *Thank you, God,* Frankie thought.

In a few minutes, Hopper emerged. Some color had returned to his face—the color green, mostly. Beads of sweat were on his brow. "I'm sorry," he said. "I wasn't expecting the odor."

"Ah, yes. It's so hot in the room. Heat accelerates decomposition," Frankie explained. He pointed the thermostat on the wall. "Look, it's set to 90 degrees. No wonder." He walked over and adjusted it.

"What do I do now?" Hopper asked. His voice trailed off.

Frankie pulled a chair out, and the officer took a seat. Frankie wrote the number for the office of the chief medical examiner and instructed the novice. "Call them. Report the death: male, Timothy Collins, approximately sixty-five years of age, under a doctor's care," he emphasized. "Tell them the doctor is on the way to pronounce him dead, and that you will call back when he does." The young officer fell back into a chair, loosened his tie, unbuttoned his top button, and began to make the call. "By the way," Frankie said, "would you mind taking possession of this?" He handed Hopper Tim's watch. "It's the only valuable I found on him." Hopper took the watch, examined it, and made notes in his book.

※

Chapter XXIX

Cardio reached down to pull a knee brace over his left knee and then another one over his right. Ace bandages were wrapped around his wrist and forearm. His trousers were on the floor. He stepped into them and dragged them up his legs. He finished dressing, swallowed four pills at his nightstand, grabbed a cane, and made his way to the Collins Agency. He pulled into the parking lot and parked alongside the police car. He cleared his throat. The air was cold and his breath visible. He left the cane in the car, walked into the office with his medical bag, and introduced himself to the police officer at the desk.

"I'm Dr. Odelli," he said to the officer. "Are you okay?" Hopper nodded "Yes" and then pointed into the office. Cardio laughed to himself as he saw how the scene had been staged. Lighting, shadows, and an odor that the officer would never forget. *Well played, Frankie.*

"He's over here, doctor," Frankie said.

Cardio walked to the corpse behind the desk, pulled rubber gloves from his bag, knelt and felt for a pulse. Frankie whispered, "This cop is a godsend." Cardio winked.

Cardio went through the motions for the benefit of Hopper, who was taking notes. He looked at his watch. He walked into the outer office and sat across from Hopper. "Have you called the medical examiner?" he asked.

The proby nodded and handed the number across the desk. Cardio dialed.

"I'm Dr. Odelli. I'm Timothy Collins' physician. I pronounced him dead at 10 p.m. He's probably been dead for three to four hours. Rigor has set in." There was a pause, and then he spoke again, responding to questions. "A massive heart attack, no doubt. I was treating him for hypertension and coronary artery disease. He had four stents in '15."

The medical examiner asked a few more questions. Cardio answered as Hopper and Frankie listened. From the doctor's conversation, Hopper gleaned that Cardio had been his doctor for 15 years. Collins had stents and a history of high blood pressure. The doctor attended the deceased just days before after an episode resulting in a visit to the emergency room. Odelli checked all the boxes the coroner required. "I'm putting you on hold," the examiner said. Hopper made notes in a black book.

Now there was a pause. Seconds seemed like hours. Frankie knew this was the key. If the coroner decided to call the body in for an autopsy, the whole plan would unravel. The next stop for Cardio and Frankie would be a holding cell. They knew many factors went into a medical examiner's decision to order an autopsy of an unattended death. Was the deceased under a doctor's care? The age, circumstances of death, medical history, and if the medical examiner was inundated with autopsies and reluctant to add one more to the workload. Especially if there was a willing doctor to attest to the cause of death.

Frankie paced back and forth. Cardio held the phone with two hands to disguise his shaking. He wondered if he was convincing.

He watched the second hand on the wall clock, silently counting along with each painstaking advance. Did the medical examiner believe him? The answer came. "No case, release number 2018–519," the coroner said. "The body is released to the undertaker." Cardio took a deep breath. It was audible. The coroner had decided not to call the body in for an autopsy, satisfied, as Cardio claimed, that the deceased died from natural causes while under a doctor's care.

Cardio hung up and reported, "The medical examiner has signed off. You can pick up the death certificate at my office in the morning, Mr. Grace."

"Thank you, Dr. Odelli," Frankie answered.

Cardio wrote a prescription for Emetrol. He handed it to Hopper. "This should help with nausea," he said. Hopper stuffed it in his pocket. Frankie sat across from the officer and called Tracy Collins. The conversation was for the benefit of Hopper, in case he was interviewed about what he saw and heard.

"Tracy," Frankie began. "Tracy, I have some bad news." He spoke slowly, as if trying to get the words out. "It's Tim. I'm sorry to tell you he's . . . passed." There was a pause. "No," Frankie said, "he wasn't shot. Doctor said it was a massive heart attack." Another pause. "Yes, yes, he's been under lots of stress." Another pause, "Yes, I guess it is better this way." He explained the circumstances. "We were going out for dinner, but he didn't answer his phone. Yes, in his office. Okay, Tracy, I'll call you in the morning to go over arrangements. Tim made pre-plans, so I'll go over the details with you."

Hopper listened to the conversation. Now Frankie had to figure a way to get him out of the office. He didn't want to take the chance that the proby would decide to step up to conquer his fear. He came up with the perfect idea. "Hey, Hopper. Do you think you can help me move the body onto my stretcher? It'll be just a minute. I have to get some spray from my van to kill maggots. Maggots all over him."

Hooper ran into the restroom. Frankie heard him regurgitating. "Maybe not," Frankie yelled. "Not to worry. I'll figure it out." Hooper came out of the restroom.

"We all finished here?" He didn't wait for an answer as he went for the door. *That went better than expected*, Frankie thought. *Maggots will do it every time.* He brought the gurney into the office, collapsed it on the floor, and placed Jane's body on it. He strapped her in, and, in minutes, he was on his way to the funeral parlor.

❊ ❊ ❊

It was after 2 a.m. when Frankie finished embalming Jane Doe. It was a service that would not ordinarily have been necessary with a pro bono case and direct cremation. But Jane had to stick around for a few more days. The embalming removed all signs of putrefaction. The internal organs were treated with cavity fluid. As he performed this process, he couldn't help but wonder out loud about her. "Who are you, Jane Doe? What went wrong in your life that led you to die alone, at a bus stop in the middle of winter? What secrets do you know?" Questions, but no answers. The odor dissipated. As he looked at her, he foresaw a problem. She was a tiny woman, frail. Her skull was small. He would have to build it up to give structure to the mask. He started to think about the options. He'd have to add another pillow or two to the torso as well.

❊ ❊ ❊

Later that morning in Frankie's office, Tim was relaxing on the couch reading *Italian for Idiots*. "You know," he said, "some of this is coming back to me. I took it in high school."

"Best six years of your life, I'm sure. By the way, I called your wife to break the news," Frankie said.

"Tracy, my Tracy. What did she say? She must have been hysterical. I know she regrets filing for divorce now. What did she say? How is she holding up?"

"She wanted to know if you'd been shot. That was her first guess."

"Mmm . . ."

"Anyway, I told her you'd made pre-arrangements and that I'd go over everything with her when we meet. I told her to bring a suit, shirt, and tie and everything you'd wear."

"Man, that must have devasted her," Tim said, more as a question.

"Hard to tell over the phone."

"Right, right," Tim agreed.

※

Chapter XXX

On Friday afternoon, Cardio had the building's porter bring corrugated boxes to his office. He asked him to come back in an hour. An ergonomic office chair was in the corner of the room. He opted instead for a motorized wheelchair to facilitate his movement around the office. He had been using it for months, more and more of late. It gave his legs a much-needed respite. The pen shook in his hand. His arm twitched as if it had a mind of its own. He guided it to the page and scribbled his signature on the last letter. His decision had been made. The letter informed his patients of his official retirement. He thanked them for their trust in him over the years and recommended three other internists for their future care. He placed the last letter in the envelope and sealed it. He looked at the bookcase, a mini-medical library. He picked up *Gray's Anatomy* and flipped through the pages. Yellow highlights brought back memories of 40 years. An array of photographs from award dinners and various galas over the years decorated the bookcase. He began removing the photographs from their frames and placing them in a box. He took an extra moment to stare at his wife's photograph, remembering the very time and place, a beach in Malibu, her hair wind-swept in an ocean breeze. He removed her picture from the frame along with others and placed them in the box. He continued taking documents and various files from his desk, filling the box. He wrote the word "Shred' on each box, using a black marker. He moved to a file cabinet and pulled his tax returns and other financial records, placing them in another box. At his fingertips was everything from his birth certificate to wedding certificate and every important document in between. From a wall safe, he took out an accordion folder titled "Dr. Claudio Odelli." He placed it in a box, leaving the safe open. He swiveled to the wall where his degrees hung. One by one, he took them from their frame and placed them in the box. His license, diploma, an honorary Doctorate from the University of Pennsylvania. There were two awards for Distinguished and Meritorious Service to Family Medicine, Internist of the Year 2009, Family Physician of the Year 2011 and 2015, and an honorary degree from the Columbia School of Medicine. One by one, he took them out of their frames and put them into a cardboard box. Exhausted, he sat and took stock. He stared, incredulous that he was able to pack his whole life into three boxes. There was another box near his desk. "Skully" was written on it. The porter returned.

"Would you bring these to my car?" he asked. He handed the man a fifty-dollar bill.

"Sure will, doctor," the man said. "What's going on? Everything okay?"

Cardio shook his head. "Yes," he answered. "For everything there is a season. I think it's about time I retired." He held up a stack of envelopes. "I'm letting all my patients know and recommending other doctors. It's time."

The porter nodded. "Well, you've been at it a long time. Best you start enjoying whatever time is left."

"Amen, brother." He looked around the office. "Amazing how much we accumulate over time."

"Ah, yes" the man said. "And it all fits in a few boxes."

"Exactly," Cardio agreed.

"I'll take care of it." He placed the boxes on a dolly and wheeled them out. "Do you want me to drop those in the mail chute?"

Cardio looked at the pile of letters in his hands. "Please do." He handed them over. He struggled to stand and reached for his coat and cane. He paused by the door for a moment and stared into the office. He flipped off the light switch and closed the door.

※

Chapter XXXI

Headlights coming across the parking lot were visible on the monitor. "It's Cardio," Frankie said. They watched as the car made a wide turn, scraping the guard rail. Then it backed up, hitting trash cans before coming to an abrupt stop near the portico. They watched Cardio pull himself out of the car. He attempted to remove a large box from the trunk. He struggled with it. "I'll help him," Tim said.

"You sit tight. We can't take the chance you're spotted. I'll go."

Frankie took the steps two at a time and ran out. "Hold on, Cardio. I got it."

Cardio sat back on the fender. "Grab that one," he said, "and bring it upstairs." He pointed to the box labeled "Skully," and Frankie lifted it out.

"What are those?" he said, pointing to the other boxes.

"I clean out my office once a year or so. I have documents shredded for safety. You can't be too careful—identity fraud and all that." The two men chuckled. "Anyway, I was thinking. You were concerned that the casket would have to have some weight. Why not place these boxes in and kill two birds with one stone?"

"Great idea, great idea. I can add to it with some of my old records," Frankie agreed. He took the boxes and stacked them in the garage.

Opting not to use the cane, Cardio took hold of Frankie's arm and clung to him. "Are you okay, Cardio?"

"Fine," Cardio assured him. "Maybe gout, that's all."

Cardio's arm entwined in Frankie's for support. Frankie walked with Cardio one painstaking step at a time. It had the same feel, the same pace as walking an octogenarian up to a casket. Once in the office, Cardio plopped down on the couch, breathing heavily. Frankie put the "Skully" box on the table, opened the box, and stared into a pile of bones. He pulled a cranium out. "Alas, poor Tim Collins. I knew him well." Cardio laughed.

"What's so funny?" Tim asked.

"Haven't you ever read Shakespeare?" Cardio asked.

"I might have," Tim answered. "Who wrote it?"

Frankie and Cardio exchanged glances. Frankie continued taking bones from the box, a femur, radial, hip. "Where did you get these?" Frankie asked.

Cardio caught his breath and ambled from the couch to a chair to the desk to the liquor cabinet. He poured a cognac and explained, "My uncle, Dr. Claudio Odelli, was a brilliant man, a graduate of Johns Hopkins."

"Now that's a medical school," Tim teased as he, too, examined the bones.

The remark was met by Cardio's middle finger. "Anyway, he moved out west, did his residency at the Mayo Clinic in Arizona. A few years later, he went into private practice. I was his only living relative. He was my idol."

Frankie was impressed as he studied the bones. "Did you get to see him often?"

"I always kept in touch with him and visited him twice a year. He was so proud when I followed in his footsteps. He was a good man. You might say everything I have, I owe to him. Anyway, he had this skeleton in his office. He called him "Skully." It was like a conversation piece. When he died, I had to go out there to finalize arrangements, clear out his office and personal effects, and settle his affairs. I took Skully apart and packed him up, maybe as a memento." Frankie handed more bones to Tim.

"Are they real?" Tim asked.

"Oh, yes. They're real human bones. They came from the Bone Room in California, probably unearthed in some desert graveyard. I know he paid a lot for him. I kept him in my office closet; I forgot he was even there until the issue came up. In retrospect, a fortunate decision. Anyway, we need him now, so here he is."

"Man," Tim said as he examined the bones. "Do you have any other skeletons in your closet?"

"This is perfect," Frankie said. "Perfect. I'll place these bones in the second casket with those boxes I take to the crematory. The boxes will add weight, and the crematory attendant will see these bone remnants when the cremation is complete. It will all look and feel normal. Perfect."

Tim had his customary blank look on his face.

Frankie explained. "During cremation, the retort hits over 2000 degrees. Everything is cremated, burnt, sent up in smoke: the casket, the body, the organs. The only remnants, what we call ashes, are actually the bone fragments and teeth that survive the flame. They are brittle and diminished but survive the flame. Those remaining bones are pulverized into the ashes. If we didn't have these, the crematory attendant would notice when he opens the retort to collect the remains. This is perfect.

Good job, Cardio." Cardio picked up his glass to acknowledge the compliment.

"So, what's the plan now?" he asked.

"Tracy is coming by tomorrow. I've got to get her to buy into this funeral plan. It's the last thing she can do for you. She's bringing your clothing. I think we should move fast. I'll place an obituary in Sunday's paper. We'll have the wake Monday and funeral mass Tuesday. After mass, I'll take Jane Doe AKA Tim Collins to the crematory. After that, I'll take Skully AKA Jane Doe; two death certificates, two cremation permits, two caskets, two bodies, two cremated remains."

"I'm dizzy," Cardio said.

"I'm hungry," Frankie said. "Let's go to Paradise and get something to eat. We'll fill Johnny in on the schedule. Nino will have to make the flight as soon as possible, maybe Monday."

"Monday?" Tim protested. "I can't leave Monday and miss my own funeral. It wouldn't feel right, me not being there and all."

Frankie shook his head. Cardio laughed. "Let's eat," he said.

Tim got up and reached for his jacket. Frankie stared at him. "Where do you think you're going?"

"I'm going with you to eat at Paradise."

Frankie shook his head. "Tim, you're already in paradise. You died at 10 p.m. last night. Sit tight. Watch television." He tossed him the remote. Cardio followed Frankie out the door as they heard Tim complaining.

"This ain't right! I'm hungry, too. I don't like being dead. It's no fun." His voice trailed off as they exited the building. "Bring me a sandwich."

Paradise Restaurant was packed. It was like the golden days. Waiters carried tables across a crowded dining room to accommodate late-night stragglers. Johnny was beaming. He motioned Frankie and Cardio to the bar. "We'd better look like we just lost our best friend," Frankie said. Johnny nodded. They exchanged hugs for show. They shook their head in disbelief. Nino took a bottle off the shelf and poured. For the benefit of those within earshot, they raised their glasses to toast their friend Tim Collins. In moments, plates of clams oreganata, eggplant rollatini, and fried calamari were followed by Capellini Putanesca. Food is an integral ingredient in Italian bereavement therapy. There were more toasts to Tim Collins, more "Remember the time when." Between melancholy reminiscences, Johnny and Nino were filled in on the timeline. Nino said he'd made flight reservations. After eating and more hugs, Frankie said goodnight and left. He returned in a moment. "Can I get a sausage and pepper sandwich to go?"

✳

Chapter XXXII

Saturday morning, Cardio came to the funeral home with bacon, egg, and cheese sandwiches. "The word is out on the street. At the deli, everyone is talking about Tim's death," he reported.

Frankie nodded. "He must have left a tab," he said with a half-smile and twitching eyebrows.

"Funny," Tim said. Then he asked, "Which deli was it? Not Philomena? We're all square."

"Actually, the phone hasn't stopped ringing here, either. People are in shock," Frankie admitted.

Tim was feeling pretty good about the early polling on his death. "What? You expected less? Come on, guys. I'm larger than life. What time is Tracy coming?" Tim asked.

"She called when you were in the shower. She'll let me know."

"There's no sense of urgency, it would seem." Cardio observed.

"Well," Frankie explained, "she had to go to the beauty parlor and then go shopping for something appropriate to wear. I told her about the timing for the wake and funeral. She's okay with it. She said the sooner, the better."

Frankie realized that didn't sound right. There was no rewording it now.

Cardio sat at Frankie's desk and filled out the medical portion of the death certificate. For the cause of death, he wrote acute myocardial infarction due to a history of arteriosclerosis, high blood pressure, and coronary artery disease. It was all true and bound to kill Tim eventually. The only item left to make the death certificate an official document was his signature and medical license number.

Frankie was standing behind him. He put his fountain pen on the desk and looked to see if he could detect any hesitation or doubt in Cardio's face. Cardio stared back, understanding this was an important moment. It was Julius Caesar crossing the Rubicon. There would be no turning back. Even at this moment, they could retreat and face minor recriminations compared to major ones. Each knew what the other was thinking. Cardio turned back and stared at the death certificate. He picked up the pen and wrote his name and license number, certifying the death of Timothy Collins.

Cardio rose, and Frankie took his seat. He completed the funeral director's portion of the death certificate, filling in the final statistical information and the time and date of disposition. He looked up at Cardio, still trying to see any doubt or second thoughts. Sensing none, he, too, affixed his signature and license number. The two men had just sealed their fate and linked their future and freedom to the successful completion of Tim's death. "I'll file it and get the permit Monday," Frankie said.

Tim was remorseful as he watched his friends. His head hung low on his chest. He understood the gravity of what their signatures on his death certificate meant and all the jeopardy he'd placed them in. "Guys," he said, "I'm so sorry. So sorry."

"It's going to be okay," Cardio said.

Frankie nodded in agreement but wasn't so sure.

✳   ✳   ✳

Later, Frankie spent time in the preparation room, trying to find the best way to build up the skull of Jane Doe so that it would support the big head of Tim Collins. The mask had to have a strong foundation, so as not to wrinkle. He settled on gauze, wrapping her skull in layers like a mummy until it formed a solid base for the mask. Then, carefully and methodically, he took the mask and put it over Jane's head. He pulled it, stretched it, and molded it; then he stepped back. With large forceps, he inserted cotton up through the neck to where more foundation was needed, each time stepping back. "Damn," he said, "damn. This just might work."

✳   ✳   ✳

At six p.m. that evening, Frankie was at the computer, writing the obituary. Cardio was napping on the couch, and Tim was sitting in a chair in his underwear, with his feet on the desk. He was reading *Italian for Idiots*. "It's coming back to me. I took this stuff in high school." Headlights came across the monitor as a car pulled into the parking lot. Everyone stared at the screen. "It's Tracy," Tim said. They watched as she took a garment and duffle bag from the car and made her way into the funeral home. Monitors caught her at the door, in the lobby, and making her way up the circular staircase to the office.

"Quick—hide," Frankie said. Cardio bumped into Tim as they made an attempt to clear the office. Tim grabbed his slacks, which were draped over a chair. Cardio grabbed his coat. There was no time to clear the glasses or bottle of Martell. They headed for the door. "No," Frankie yelled. "She's coming up the stairs." He pointed to the louvered doors that led to the living quarters. "Go in there—quick!"

The two men rushed through the doors just as Tracy appeared at the office door. They settled in and peeked through the louvers. She looked stunning, bathed in the soft office lights. She was wearing a full-length mink. Her hair was coiffed; earrings, a mixture of diamond and ruby, glimmered. Frankie moved toward her. It was the first time he'd seen her since Tim's death. He gave her a hug; "I'm so sorry," he said. "It's like a bad dream. Are you okay? Come in, come in." He took the garment bag and duffle bag.

Tracy sashayed across the room and sat in the very chair Tim had vacated moments earlier. "I'm fine," she said. "The phone hasn't stopped ringing. People are shocked. I guess he was under too much stress. The police came to my house this morning. Considering what he was facing—not to mention what I'm facing—I guess this was best."

"Maybe," Frankie agreed.

"Anyway, I brought two sports jackets and slacks. He seldom wore suits. Choose the outfit you think is best. His undergarments and shoes are in there. There's a turtleneck. He didn't wear dress shirts and hated ties. So, I brought a scarf if you think it works." She pointed to the duffle. "To be honest, Frankie, I feel very uncomfortable. Tim must have told you I filed for divorce. I don't know if I should even be involved with his funeral."

"Tracy . . ."

"No, Frankie—you don't understand. I'm in legal trouble. I trusted him. I signed documents he put in front of me. He signed my name on others. I'm just as guilty as he is, in the eyes of the law. Dropping dead might have been the nicest thing he ever did for me. That's what my cousin told me."

"Your cousin?"

"Bernie Schwartz. He's my lawyer."

Frankie needed to navigate this. "Well, Tracy, I know you've had problems. But I also know Tim. He must have felt he could work his way out of this situation. He just ran out of time. I'm sure he did not mean to put you in legal jeopardy. It would have been the last thing he wanted."

"But he did, and I am. I want nothing more to do with him. My cousin says I'm in unimaginable debt and legal jeopardy. I don't know what to do. If he was here, I'd kill him myself."

"Tracy, why not just get through the next few days? You're still married and all. Now that he's dead, maybe the feds will rethink your culpability. They'd have nothing to gain by pursuing you. They were squeezing him, hoping to snare bigger fish. He's gone; he can't help them anymore; neither can you."

She sat back in the chair, contemplating the suggestion.

Frankie kept up the sales pitch. "He kind of made all his arrangements when he had the heart problem. He didn't think he'd survive and did not want to burden you with making his funeral arrangements. That's how much he loved you. Just go through the motions. What's the harm at this point?"

"I don't know," she said. "I'm confused."

"Tracy," Frankie cajoled, "one last gesture, for the good years."

"Both of them?" she asked.

Frankie smiled. "Two out of ten ain't bad." Tracy smiled, too. "Tracy, what do you say?"

"Well, if you think so," she said. "You were always so level-headed. I wish he was more like you."

Frankie nodded. "He was one of a kind, that's for sure. What do you say, Tracy?"

"You really think I should?"

"I do," he said. "You know, Tim came to me just before he had his stents put in. He was concerned about you even back then. He made all his wishes known. If you can see your way to just get though the next few days."

Tracy nodded. She pulled a silk handkerchief from her sleeve and dabbed her eyes.

"I guess," she said. "What were his wishes?"

"Basically, he wanted a one-day wake, then a mass at St. Catherine, followed by cremation."

She looked up. "Cremation? That's odd. We went to a funeral with a cremation once, and he wasn't happy. 'Not for me,' he said. "It's like paying respects to a spittoon. Maybe I should bury the bastard."

Frankie wasn't expecting this. It was problematic. A body buried would ultimately bury him and Cardio as well. It could be exhumed and tested for DNA. He had to talk her out of it and make it seem like her idea.

"Well, it would be against his wishes." He showed her the file. "I guess you can buy a grave. A plot will be costly, though. Maybe five thousand dollars plus another thousand to open the grave and another thousand for a vault and another few thousand for a monument."

Her fingers moved like she was playing a piano. She was doing the math. "I guess if he said cremation, we should follow his wishes. It's only right. It's cheaper, too. I'm broke. I can't afford a funeral, especially one that he'd planned for himself."

Frankie jumped in. "Not an issue. His friend Johnny has already called to tell me he'd help with expenses. He's got some friends to kick in, too. We'll keep it simple but dignified. Nothing extravagant."

"Like some kind of an Italian Go Fund Me thing?" She took a deep breath.

Frankie's insides were shaking. "I think you're doing the right thing." She dabbed her eyes. Then the unthinkable happened. Frank Sinatra was singing, "Fly Me to the Moon." Frankie's face went pale. There, on the desk right in front of Tracy, was Tim's phone, wallet, car keys and a box of cigars. Frankie was muttering, stumbling, "I, I'm so sorry Tracy. I had Tim's personal effects . . ." He reached for the phone and declined the call, fumbling for the button. "I'm so sorry." He swept the items into a desk drawer.

"It's okay," she said, reaching for the wallet. "I'm sure it wasn't easy for you." She ran her fingers delicately along the snakeskin, back and forth, back and forth. She opened the wallet as she spoke. "Yes, we should follow his wishes," she said as she smoothly removed bills from the wallet, stuffing them into her coat pocket. "Do you know when we will have the death certificates?"

Enough grieving; let's get down to business, Frankie thought. "Sure. I'll have them Monday."

She sobbed and dabbed her eyes. "Will they be certified? Bernard says they should be certified."

"Yes, they will be certified."

She dabbed her eyes. "Am I entitled to Social Security death benefits?"

Frankie scratched his head. "Well, you'd be entitled when you reach the age of sixty-two."

"Not before?" She dabbed her eyes.

"No, and it may have to be split with his first two wives."

"What?" She stopped dabbing.

"Yes," Frankie said. "But you do get two hundred and fifty-five dollars as a death benefit."

"That's all?" she asked, as she dabbed her eyes again. "It doesn't sound like such a benefit."

"Yes, that's what it is," Frankie said. "I'll fill out all the papers for you."

She sobbed again and dabbed her eyes. "Do you know anyone who wants to buy his car? It hardly has any mileage. I don't know why he bought a Jaguar. His change-of-life car. Tim Tosterone."

"Not offhand," Frankie said. "But we'll figure something out."

She stood up, and Frankie came around the desk. "You've been so good. I know you lost a dear, dear friend."

"He was like a brother."

She nodded. Frankie was standing near her now. "Thank you, Frankie." She leaned in to kiss his cheek. He immediately felt something, a sixth sense, an innate feeling. Something about that little kiss on the cheek. Maybe it was the moistness, the tenderness; maybe it lingered a millisecond longer. Maybe his imagination? Then there was another as she stepped closer to him. He backed up toward the couch as she approached. Then another kiss, full lip lock. Her hands wrapped around his head, holding it like a vise. He backed up, falling onto the couch. Then, his own phone rang. He reached for it. "Yes dear," he said. At that moment, Tracy's mink fell from her shoulders. She stood there, immersed in moonlight, wearing a bustier from Victoria's Secret. It molded her breasts, shaped her hips, and left Frankie stuttering. "Ya, ya, ya, yes, dear," he said into the phone. "No, I don't know the number of the exterminator."

Tracy fell to her knees, attacking his zipper. With his free hand he moved to block her. "Well, geckos are not a real problem." She went for his buckle. He moved to block her. "Yes, but they are harmless." The tug-o-war between zipper and belt buckle continued for what seemed like an eternity. His breathing was audible;

his words got caught in his throat. "No, no," he said, "I'm, I'm fine. Yes, you heard about Tim. Yes, tragic. No, not cirrhosis—a heart attack." Frankie struggled valiantly to maintain composure and protect his family jewels. "Hey, honey, can I get back to you? Something's come up."

Beyond the louvered doors Cardio could hardly contain Tim. He had one arm wrapped around him and the other hand across his mouth. Frankie rolled off the couch. "I'll call you tomorrow. Yes—love you, too."

He fell off the couch and crawled to the mink, with her clinging to him. He struggled to his feet. Tracy stood up, and he covered her with the coat. "Tracy, Tracy, now, calm down. You're not thinking right. You're under stress. You're not thinking straight."

She put on her coat. "I'm sorry," she said. She leaned in and planted one more kiss on his lips. He stood frozen as she made her way out of the office. Just then Cardio and Tim fell through the doors. Cardio remained supine, gasping for air, half choking, half laughing, exhausted from his struggle with Tim.

"Jesus Christ!" Tim yelled. "I'm not dead one day and you're strufin' my wife." He grabbed the book and flipped through the pages. *"Disgrazia!"* he said, pointing.

Frankie was still reeling. "Tim, calm down. People grieve differently."

He looked in the book again. *"Puttana!* And you, my best friend." Frankie was at a loss for words. Cardio was choking on his laughter.

"That two-timing . . . *Puttana!* I guess all those rumors were true. And she files for divorce. That two-timing . . . I'm glad I changed my beneficiary. I had second thoughts after she broke the news in the hospital, but I'm glad I did it now. I mean, what kind of woman tells you she filed for divorce after you almost got killed?"

"Papers like that need to be notarized and witnessed," Frankie said.

"I know. I forged your name and borrowed your notary seal."

Frankie was still visibly shaken. He exchanged glances with Cardio. "I need some air," he said.

Cardio had crawled to the desk and lifted himself up. "Let's get dinner. It's on me."

Tim grabbed his jacket. Frankie stopped him. "Do I have to remind you? You're dead, remember? Sit tight; have a drink."

"I hate you. And you, too," he said pointing to Cardio. "I don't like being dead."

Cardio and Frankie left the office. Tim yelled after them. "*Traditore*! Bring me a sandwich. You better not be meeting my wife. That *Puttana*! Sausage and peppers."

*

Chapter XXXIII

O*n Sunday morning, Frankie finalized* the death certificate for Jane Doe. The public administrator of the county was the authorizing party, and the medical examiner was the doctor of record. Other than that, there was little information to be written on the certificate; no name of parents, no place of birth, no marital status or education. *Jane Doe was just a poor soul who seemed to fall through the cracks,* he thought.

Tim had calmed down. Cardio brought donuts and coffee. "The whole town is shocked," he said. "They can't believe you're dead." He'd brought the Sunday paper as well. Tim went to the obituary page.

"How many people get to read their own obituary?" he quipped. He read aloud.

"Timothy Collins, of Inlet Cove, died suddenly February 15, 2018. He was sixty-six years old. Timothy was founder of the Collins Real Estate Development and Brokerage Agency. Beloved husband of Tracy (nee Schwartz). To honor his life, friends may call at the Grace Funeral Home 767 Cove Rd. Inlet Cove on Monday from 4 to 8 pm. A mass of Christian Burial will be held on Tuesday 11 a.m. at St. Catherine's R.C. Church. Committal will be private. For more information or to place an online condolence, www.gracefuneralhome.com' Tim looked up. "A little skimpy, don't you think?"

"I embellished on the one your wife wrote," Frankie said.

"What did she write?"

Frankie picked up a random piece of paper and read, "Tim Collins dead at 66. Car for sale." Cardio doubled up with laughter, as Tim threw a jelly donut at Frankie and a creampuff at Cardio.

※

Chapter XXXIV

*L*ater that afternoon, it was time to prepare for Monday's wake. Frankie looked into the garment bag. There were two outfits inside. "Pick one," he said.

Tim looked at each. "I like this blue jacket with gray pants. Maybe I'll wear it to Italy. Use this one." He handed the black jacket to Frankie. Tracy had brought a white turtleneck and a scarf. "What do you think?" Frankie asked, laying it across the black jacket.

"Sharp," Tim said. "Elegant grunge. I want to look good. There should be a lot of chickiepoos attending." He winked. "I want to look my best."

"Did you actually say *chickiepoos*?" Frankie opened the duffle bag. There were socks and a pair of black suede shoes.

Tim looked at the shoes. "Is she kidding? I'm not burning these. These are Bruno Magli. I'll wear them."

Frankie put the shoes in the bag and pulled out an undershirt and then, with two fingers, a pair of tighty whities. "Really," he said.

Tim grabbed them from his hand. "Don't judge."

Frankie was busy in the embalming room. It was time to dress Tim. He used duct tape to keep the pillows in place and wrapped sheets around Jane Doe's body to add more bulk. Tim's clothing had to fit. He put plastic protective garments on her as well.

Upstairs, Tim was going stir crazy, stuck in the office. He ventured down to the main floor. Flower pieces had arrived—quite a few, too. He heard a motor and followed the sound. He opened a door and saw a casket coming up through the floor. The floor lift stopped. Then he heard footsteps coming from below.

"Tim, you can't be here. What if someone sees you? Are you crazy?"

"Yeah, I am. I'm going nuts up there."

Frankie walked around the funeral home and locked all the doors. "Come with me," he said. He positioned Tim on the foot end of the casket and rolled it off the lift, through the lobby, and into the chapel. Tim examined the casket, knocking on the wood. "Is this any good? I don't want to be embarrassed."

"It's solid oak. You don't deserve it." Frankie centered the casket and switched on lights.

"Is this the room I'm going to be in? Do you think it's big enough?"

"This is the room. Sit here," he said. Tim sat in a leather armchair in the front row. He stretched his legs and leaned back into the soft cushion. In a moment, Frankie came in, rolling a cart with an array of grooming tools, cotton rolls, Vaseline, and various jars of cosmetics. He opened the casket. Tim nearly fell off the chair. He stared in disbelief at the body in the casket. There in his jacket, his shirt and scarf, his socks, his shoes, his head, and, possibly, his tighty-whities was . . . him.

"Holy mother Macree! This is totally unreal." He stepped closer. "Frankie, this is incredible."

"I'm not finished, either." He stepped back to look from a distance. "Sit down, Tim. I've got work to do."

Tim sat back in the chair and watched Frankie. First, he studied Tim's face. "Ruddy," he said out loud. He looked through the bottles and settled on one, pouring its contents into a small hand-held apparatus, the size of a flashlight. A small nozzle extended from it. Then, with the steadiest of hands, he moved it across the bald head, holding the nozzle gingerly between two fingers, like an artist. A light mist of cosmetic began to cover the head, the flow controlled by pressure from his finger, like a dentist's drill. Slowly, evenly, he moved the spray across the cheekbones, jawline, and chin. Tim watched in amazement as, with each layer of mist, he came to life. The coloring was impeccable. No brushstrokes.

"Incredible," Tim said. "I'm impressed. You're an artist."

"Not finished. That's just the base. Looks good, though," Frankie said. He poured from another bottle and began again, this time highlighting the cheekbones with hints of rouge that added contour, layer upon layer. When he was finished, he stepped back to admire his work. He looked into the casket, and he looked at Tim. "I'm good," he said. From a plastic bag, he carefully extracted the eyebrow clippings that The Chef had cut. Meticulously, using a tweezers, he embedded them above the eye sockets, adhering them with the tiniest speckle of mortuary wax. Then the *piece de resistance*: he placed Tim's toupee, adjusting it left, right, up, down. He combed it out.

They stood side by side, looking at Jane Doe, the body double of Timothy Collins.

They were one and the same. "Jesus, I look good," Tim said. "Looks like I'm sleeping. So peaceful. But, my hair, I don't like it. It looks like a toupee. No one knows I wear a piece."

Frankie looked at him. "You're kidding, right?"

"No. You got to fix it."

Frankie made some adjustments as Tim looked on. When the building's boiler kicked in, fans blew hot air through the overhead vents, causing Tim's hair to flutter up over his forehead.

"Please, Frankie you got to fix that." Tim said again. "I'll die from embarrassment."

Frankie laughed.

"What's so funny?"

"I was just remembering my father. He had the same problem once."

"How did he solve it?"

Frankie put the hairbrush on the tray and looked at Tim. "A nail," he said.

Now, only the hands were left. Frankie slipped the polymer gloves over her hands and went to work with the air gun. When he was finished, he entwined a pair of rosary beads between her fingers.

"This is going to give me nightmares," Tim said. "Something wrong with seeing yourself dead. Something wrong."

"Do you think it will fool everyone?" Frankie asked.

He looked at Frankie. "Keep it open," he said, echoing The Chef's words.

"You'd better get back upstairs. I've got to unlock the doors. Flower deliveries will be coming."

Tim backed up slowly, never taking his eyes off him in the casket, bumping into every piece of furniture on the way out.

Frankie unlocked the flower door as a floral-delivery van pulled in. "Hi, Frankie. Sorry about Tim. He was a character," the delivery man said. He took a large cuneiform-shaped floral piece from the van. "Should I leave it here in the flower room, Frankie?"

Frankie thought this would be a good test. "Would you mind bringing it into the chapel?"

"No problem." The man carried it into the reposing room and placed it next to the casket as Frankie looked on. The man paused a moment and stared at Tim in the casket. Frankie was nervous at his reaction, but there was none. But, then the delivery man bowed his head, knelt down, whispered a prayer, and then made the sign of the cross.

Frankie sighed. He'd passed the first test. "Hard to believe," the man said as he left. "We lost a good customer. He was always sending roses to someone. Anyway, he looks great. Hard to believe."

Frankie went to his office. Tim was behind the desk, watching the monitor. "We're ready for Broadway," he said.

Chapter XXXV

Frankie was surprised at the number of flowers that were delivered. He knew Tim had many friends, but this was overwhelming. The reposing room was inundated with unique standing floral sprays and baskets. They were unique specialty floral pieces that included a pair of dice, a slot machine, four aces, a king of diamonds, a joker, a roulette table, a football, a baseball and bat, a bicycle, a nearly full-sized stallion, boxing gloves, a formula-one race car, and a greyhound, all made from utilizing the full spectrum of horticultural flowers. Frankie started to notice a theme. The pieces reflected the array of Tim's extracurricular interests. The cards attached to the pieces were names Frankie didn't recognize. There was Ziggy, and Ingy, Louie, Fritzie, Buster, Bruno, a "friend," as well as from dealers and staff and coat-check girls from hotels from Vegas to Atlantic City and jockeys from every racetrack in between. Frankie shook his head in disbelief, realizing his friend operated in a different world. There was also a small spray for the bottom of the casket. "Husband" was on the ribbon.

✳

Chapter XXXVI

At three o'clock on Monday, Nino came to the office. Cardio had just arrived as well but did not make the flight up to the office. "The doctor is downstairs," Nino reported. "My uncle went to pick up Tracy. They should be here at any moment."

"It's showtime," Frankie said to Tim. On the monitor, they could see police cars and news crews setting up around the perimeter. It had the appearance of an opening night on Broadway.

"This is incredible," Tim observed.

"I can pack a room, can't I?"

"This is probably the most exciting thing that happened in Inlet Cove in about . . . forever," Frankie agreed. As he had predicted, the local news finally had a real story right in their midst. Tim's arrest and untimely death was big news in a small town. Interviewing the recipient of Rotary's "Perfect Attendance" award would have to wait.

Reporters spoke with mourners as police kept traffic moving. There were flares in the street, and strobe lights from the police cars were crisscrossing the sky, giving it the feel of Academy Award night in Hollywood. A cadre of federal agents were taking pictures as well. All visitors would be part of their database. A black Escalade pulled into the parking lot. Men bounded from the front and rear seats and assisted another man from the vehicle. "It's Napoli," Frankie said. They watched as one of the men lit Napoli's cigarette.

"Ah, that's nice of him to come," Tim said. "He's so respectful."

"You're oblivious, aren't you? He's not here to pay his respects. He's here to make sure you're dead. Sit tight. Do not leave this room. I repeat, don't leave this room. Hopefully, we will get through this night. Go. Sit," he ordered.

Nino followed Frankie down the staircase. Cardio was waiting at the bottom. He had a cane in each hand and was leaning against the banister. "What the hell?" Frankie exclaimed.

Cardio waved him off. "I twisted my knee struggling with that mook last night. I'm fine."

Cars were pulling into the parking lot, and people were gathering in the lobby. The doors to the reposing room were closed. "How does he look?" Cardio asked.

"Actually, he never looked so good," Frankie answered.

Johnny Paradise called Frankie on his cell phone. "We're pulling in," he reported.

"They're here," Frankie announced. He checked the lighting in the room. The dimmer the better. Back in the lobby, he waited as Johnny walked Tracy into the funeral home. She was wearing the same mink. Frankie thought twice about helping her with her coat, afraid of what she might be wearing—or not wearing—underneath. She saved him the decision by whisking it off her shoulders and handing it to him. She was wearing a red knit dress that clung to every contour of her body. "Restroom?" the lady in red asked. No one answered as they stood with their mouths open. "Restroom?" She said again. Frankie pointed as he took a deep breath. All three men watched as she floated toward the lavatory.

Johnny asked Nino, "Did you bring them?"

Nino reached for the aluminum foil in his pocket. He unraveled it, revealing small peppers. "Eat one of these," he said.

Frankie and Cardio looked at him in disbelief. He explained, "These will keep us from laughing, and, in no time at all, we'll have tears streaming down our face. They measure 20,000 on the Scoville scale. It's the only way."

Everyone remembered the last time they ate peppers like this. They looked at each other. Frankie was first, followed by Cardio, Nino, and Johnny. The popped the peppers into their mouths as Tracy exited the restroom. Frankie's face was already on fire; he couldn't breathe.

Upstairs, Tim was watching on the monitor in Frankie's office. *She's in red*, he thought. *For Valentine's day*, he assumed.

For Frankie, walking a family up to the casket for the first time was among the most stressful aspects of his profession. He'd performed this unenviable duty thousands of times over his career, and it still gave him the shakes. First reactions ranged from "Good job," to "That's not him. The hair is all wrong," to "That's not her nose." After initial shock wears off, reality sets in, denial turns to acceptance. But those first moments caused Frankie heart palpitations. In this case, Tracy would be looking at a mask. Her reaction could be either the first step to prison for him and Cardio or the crucial validation that would allow the wake to proceed.

Frankie held her arm as they walked into the room and toward the casket. His experience had prepared him for everything—a wife jumping into the casket to hug her husband, kisses that would undo hours of cosmetic work. In this case, especially, that would be problematic. He remained vigilant, knowing that there was not much left of their marriage and that, if she did jump on Tim, it might only be to strangle him for leaving her in a financial and criminal mess. He was ready to hold her back. She stood a few feet back from the kneeler. "I've never done this before. I like our way better: Bing, bang, boom—where's the Shiva," she said. She stared at the body. "Do you think we should close the casket?"

Frankie didn't anticipate that request. A closed casket would raise all kinds of suspicions. He had to be delicate. "I know this is not in keeping with your Jewish tradition, but all Tim's friends have come to pay respects. It's important for them to say goodbye. After all, if it's closed, it will be like asking them to pay their respects to a credenza. Kind of pointless, don't you agree?"

She tossed her head back and forth, weighing the case for an open casket. "Whatever," she said. "What am I supposed to do now?"

"You can say a prayer," Frankie suggested. "*Kaddish*, maybe?" His felt the heat in his face. He started coughing and gagging as tears formed.

"Are you alright?" she asked. She wiped tears from his eyes. Cardio, Johnny, and Nino were behind them, all suffering from the effects of the peppers. She looked at them. "I know, you were good friends. His homies. Where should I sit?"

Frankie escorted her to the front row. She sat in the same chair that Tim was sitting in the day before as he watched Frankie work. "Friends will begin to come in to offer their condolences."

She nodded. Johnny and Nino were first to kneel at the casket. There were moans coming from them as they fought the effects from the hot peppers. Eyes watered; tears poured down their faces. It was the first time they'd seen the finished product, and, if not for the peppers making them cry, they might well be laughing. Cardio stood behind them, opting not to kneel. He, too, was suffering from the peppers.

The trio was complimentary. "Great job, Frankie. He looks great." Johnny said, "I mean for being dead and all." He blew his nose, coughed, and cried.

Cardio observed, "Doesn't look like he belongs in there. Like he wants to talk to us or crack a joke or something."

Nino's voice was cracking. "Looks just like him," he said. This drew stares from everyone.

"Why wouldn't it?" Tracy asked. "It wasn't like he was sick or anything."

Johnny helped. "No, I go to wakes where they do a terrible job. You don't even recognize the person. Tim looks great. So real, so lifelike, natural."

Tracy nodded. They took seats a few rows behind her, grabbing a box of tissues as well.

There was a steady flow of people during the visiting hours. Frankie knew most of them—locals, friends. There were cocktail waitresses and barmaids from every restaurant within 30 miles. The best men and wedding parties from the three weddings came. Marco and the busboys and cooks from Paradise's Restaurant knelt, prayed, and cried real tears. Marco was really shaken. He took a seat next to Tracy and hugged her for a long time. She stroked his head to console him. A Pop football team that Tim sponsored came in as a group. Two ominous Asian men waited patiently in line. They approached the casket, whispered to each other, and left. They did not look happy, but, after all, it was a wake. Three other men, one with a disfiguring facial scar along his left cheek, also approached the casket. Frankie heard them talking in a thick accent. *I think I just met Sergi*, he thought. And not to be outdone, Reno Amore showed up with a contingent of agents. Amore looked more like an undertaker than Frankie. He was somber, pale, with an unwelcoming face. He stood in line, waiting to approach the casket as his agents spread around the room. Some were copying the names from the cards on the flower pieces. Others engaged in conversation with visitors. Amore didn't kneel at the casket. He just stared for an inordinate amount of time—stared and stared, and then he scratched his mustache, turned toward Tracy, and nodded in her direction. He passed the red-faced Frankie, with his bloodshot eyes and a runny nose. "You lost a good friend," he said.

Frankie struggled to find his voice. His throat was on fire, sore. "He was," he said. "He was the best."

Amore looked directly into Frankie's eyes. He said nothing, just nodded and walked away, surveying the room.

Frankie watched the visitors milling about the room, gathering in small groups to talk about everything from the weather to vacations, to car purchases to movies they just saw. Life goes on. Tim was history already; the memory stage had begun. In the line, he also saw a small man with a cane limping toward the casket. It was The Fixer himself. He was escorted by a buxom blonde, who towered over him. *That Strega works*, Frankie thought. The Chef didn't kneel. He simply stared at the body. Then he turned toward Frankie and winked. He approached Tracy. "You don't know me," he said. "I only met your husband once, and he made quite an impression on me. I had to come to see him."

"You're so kind. Thank you, Mr.?"

"Chef—they call me Chef."

Napoli was more traditional. He knelt and made the sign of the cross. Frankie's heart pounded when he reached into the casket to pat the body a few times. With each pat, Frankie gagged. A mannequin would have been a dead giveaway. Satisfied, Napoli went to Tracy, extended his hand, and kissed her. There was a little conversation before he walked away. Napoli then turned toward Frankie and motioned him to the side of the room.

"Tell me, Frankie. You picked him up from his office?" As Napoli spoke, his eyes were focused like a laser on Tim in the casket.

"Yes, Sam. We were supposed to have dinner. He didn't answer the phone, so I went over there and found him."

"Then you called Odelli?"

Frankie thought before answering. "No, I called the police, and they called the medical examiner. Then I called his doctor, Odelli."

"Let me ask you: Did he have any money on him?"

"Money?"

"Yeah, money."

"A few dollars in his wallet, as I recall. I gave it to Tracy."

"No, I mean *real* money." Frankie shook his head. "Would you believe this degenerate hit two of my street guys up for a loan? That was Thursday about four or five o'clock. He borrowed $4K from one and $6K from the other." Frankie felt Napoli's eyes staring right through him now, looking for the smallest clue. "Can you tell me where $10K would go in a matter of hours?"

Frankie started stuttering. "I . . . don't know. There was nothing in the office or in his pocket. I swear, Mr. Napoli."

"What about her?" he said, motioning toward Tracy. "Have you been paid for the funeral? Perhaps with new $100 bills?"

"No, sir, no. She doesn't have a clue. I don't think she even realizes the extent of her financial situation."

He nodded, staring at Tim. "I feel like ripping that degenerate's head off, just to send a message." He made a small move toward the casket. "Maybe I will."

Frankie gulped and swallowed hard. He felt his heart trying to get out of his chest.

❊   ❊   ❊

From his bird's-eye seat in Frankie's office Tim watched the monitors, giving play-by-play commentary. His comments ranged from, "Get that bastard away from my wife," to "I can't believe he had the nerve to come," to "Not a bad crowd."

As the 8 p.m. hour approached, the crowd had diminished. The television cameras had packed up. Tim was excited to watch the 10 p.m. news. The police cars had left as well. "Do I have to stay until the end?" Tracy asked.

"No, I guess not. Most people have left," Frankie said, "and you must be exhausted. Plus, tomorrow is another big day. Best you get some rest. I'll have a limousine pick you up in the morning at 10:30 and take you to St. Catherine's. You get some rest."

"Will you give the eulogy?" she asked.

"No. I'm not good at talking to a live audience. I think Cardio has put something together."

"Tell him to keep it brief," she said. "Less is more." Frankie walked Tracy to the door and said goodnight, from a distance. Johnny took her by the arm. Nino and Cardio sat in the lobby as Frankie switched off the lights in the chapel and locked all the doors. "Can you believe it? Can you believe we got through it?" Nino asked.

"I wonder how he's doing?" Cardio pointed upstairs.

"Let's go see," Nino said.

"Yeah, I've got to give him a piece of my mind," Frankie said.

Nino and Frankie helped Cardio up the stairs. They found Tim sitting behind Frankie's desk. "This was reality television," he said. "Incredible. I'm so proud at the turnout."

"You stupid son of a bitch," Frankie yelled.

"What?"

"You hit up Napoli for $10K? Are you crazy? Out of your mind?"

"I gave it to Nino," he said. "We need euros."

"I can't believe this." Frankie slumped in a chair. "He wants to kill you. He's looking for the money. Wants to know where you could have spent it so quickly. He wants to make an example of you."

"Relax, Frankie. Besides, it's too late to kill me. I'm dead. Being dead ain't so bad. It's liberating. I'm sorry." He poured a drink.

"It's true, Frankie. I bought euros," Nino said. "We are all set to leave tomorrow, JFK to Rome."

※

Chapter XXXVII

Later that night, Frankie was in the embalming room. He rolled another oak casket into the embalming room After taking Jane Doe AKA Timothy Collins to the crematory, he would arrange for another hearse to bring this casket with the bones. That would complete the circle. Two caskets, two permits, two death certificates, two cremated remains. That was the plan.

Frankie placed Skully's bones in the oak casket, forming the outline of a human body. Then, one by one, he placed the boxes from Cardio's office into the casket. They added much-needed weight. The last box slipped from his hands, its contents spilling across the floor. "Damn it," he said. He began retrieving all the papers, piece by piece, placing them back into the folder marked "Dr. Claudio Odelli." Without realizing it, he was absorbing bits and pieces of the file's contents. He looked again at the file. He felt guilty, betraying a trust, snooping, but, reluctantly, he continued. Something was very strange. The file was extensive and chronicled the career of Cardio's uncle.

From the corner of his eye, he caught movement on the monitor. Headlights were coming through the parking lot. Thinking nothing of it, he continued to study the file. In a few minutes, the car circled again and stopped. The hair on his neck rose. Two men in ski masks got out of the car. The car eased away. One was carrying a small medical bag. They came to the back door and then moved around the building, from one monitor to the other. Frankie couldn't believe what he was thinking. Napoli wanted Tim's scalp, and it had to be attached to Tim's head. He had to send a message. Frankie stuffed the file back into the box, put it into the casket, and closed the lid. He ran upstairs to the reposing room and closed the casket's lid. By instinct, he rolled the casket through the dark room, between folding chairs, end tables, couches, and flowers. Once in the lobby, he steered the casket into the flower room, onto the floor lift, and then into the basement preparation room behind a locked door. If Napoli's men got into the funeral home, they would go home empty-handed. He followed them on the screens as they moved from one entry point to another.

He called the Inlet Cove police. The desk officer was Mallory. "Chuck, it's Frankie Grace."

"Evening, Mr. Grace. You had some crowd there tonight."

"Yes, nice turnout for Tim."

"I guess a lot of people wanted to make sure he was dead. Word on the street is that the boys are not too happy with his death—by natural causes that is." He laughed at his own joke. "What can I do for you?"

"Would you mind sending a car? I think someone might be trying to get into the funeral home."

"A ghoul, huh? Looking for a souvenir."

"Yeah, probably." *Most certainly, something for over the mantel.*

"A unit is on the way," Mallory said. In the tense moments that followed, Frankie monitored all the cameras around the funeral home. Two figures crossed the lobby, coinciding with the screech of a siren getting louder and louder. A police car pulled into the parking lot. *I hope it's not Hopper. Please, not Hopper,* Frankie thought. The officer approached the back door as the two silhouettes made a quick exit out the front door, empty-handed, headless.

Frankie took a deep breath. He made his way to the main floor and switched on lights. He yelled out to the patrolman.

"Are you okay, Mr. Grace?" the officer responded.

"Yes, yes, I'm fine. It was probably nothing. My imagination, maybe."

The officer moved around with flashlight in hand. "I don't think so, Mr. Grace."

He pointed the flashlight to some broken glass on the floor. "Someone was here—broke the window to unlock the door."

Frankie knew as much. "I can't believe it," he said. "Nothing is sacred. Kids, no doubt."

"Probably. Anyway, I'll keep an eye out tonight. I'll make a few passes on my tour."

"I appreciate that."

* * *

Tim was sound asleep on the couch in Frankie's office. Frankie poured himself a drink and stared at his friend in peaceful slumber. *What a night,* he thought. He sat behind his desk and assessed the plan. So far, so good. The hearse would arrive in the morning. A limousine was ordered to take Tracy to the church, and another would take Nino and Tim to JFK. Timing would be key. He put his feet up on the desk and thought about Tim's future with Nino. He thought about his friend Johnny Paradise, and he thought about his friend, Doctor Claudio Odelli.

Frankie was up early. He moved the casket back into the reposing room. He arranged for some flowers to be brought to church
in advance.

※　※　※

Later that morning, a limousine pulled into the parking area
of Paradise's Restaurant. The driver helped Nino with his luggage.
Frankie thought a limousine on the morning of the funeral would
not seem out of place. The next stop was the funeral home. In the
office upstairs, Frankie and Tim were monitoring the scene in the
chapel. Tim was biting his nails, finally showing signs of concern.

Johnny picked up Cardio, and they all met in Frankie's office.
The mood was funereal; the room was quiet as the men realized
that this would be the last time they would see their friend. It was
a wake in every sense—the last goodbye. It was no different from
the thousands of times Frankie had stood by a casket with a family member, knowing this was the last time they would ever see
their loved one. Tim Collins was no more. Tears were welling up
in Frankie's eyes, Cardio was sniffling, and Johnny, too. Hot peppers were not needed.

"Listen." Frankie could hardly talk. "You're 'Luciano Greco'
now. Don't muck it up."

Tim nodded and took the pouch from Frankie. It contained his
new identity. "I won't. I promise." He could hardly speak. "I want
to thank you guys. I'll never be able to thank you for all you did.
I'm sorry, sorry I put all of you in this."

On the monitor, they saw a hearse pull into the parking lot.
Frankie looked at his watch. "We'd better get moving." The moment
had come to say goodbye. They stood side by side, fighting the

emotion. It would not take much for the grown men to break down. Johnny was first to embrace Tim. "Be good. Stay out of trouble. If that's possible," he added. Tears were uncontrollable. "Keep your eye on him," he told Nino.

Cardio rose. "Goodbye, Tim. Take care of yourself. Get a doctor over there, and follow his instructions." The embrace lingered. Tim was bawling. He felt Cardio's weight in his arms.

For as many times as Frankie had to say goodbye to someone he knew and cared about, this would be most difficult. This had all the makings of a real funeral. Tim was as good as dead. Forever gone from his orbit, the very definition of death. Tim spoke first as Frankie approached.

"Frankie . . ."

Frankie waved him off. His voice cracked. "Don't say anything. Don't," he said, knowing a spoken word would reduce both to rubble. The two embraced. After an eternity, Frankie stepped back and cupped Tim's face in his palms as if to study it for one last time, to embed the image in his brain, so he'd be able to recall the last moment, the face, the friend. Satisfied, he turned to Johnny and Cardio. "Let's go," he said. "We don't want to be late for his funeral."

The three men walked down into the lobby. Johnny held Cardio as he labored with the steps. Entering the lobby was Reno Amore and six agents from central casting, each carrying their obligatory coffee container, each looking like they'd slept in their suits.

"Good morning, Mr. Grace."

"Not really," Frankie said. "Can I help you?"

"No, we are here to attend a funeral." He walked over to Johnny. "I'm agent Reno Amore. We've met before?"

Johnny nodded. "Johnny Paradise. I'm a friend of the family. We met at the hospital when Tim was rushed there."

Amore nodded and looked to Cardio. "Hello," the doctor said. "We've met, too. I'm Dr. Odelli. I'm Tim's doctor."

Amore's eyebrows twitched. "You mean, you *were* his doctor," Amore said. "The very doctor who signed his death certificate, if I'm not mistaken. Well, gentlemen, don't let us get in your way."

Frankie led Cardio and Johnny up to the casket. As stressful as it always was for Frankie to walk a family to a casket for the first time, it was equaled by being with them when, for the last time, they say goodbye. Johnny knelt. Cardio stood behind him. Each felt the stare of Amore and company. "I'll see you in church," Frankie said. Johnny and Cardio made the sign of the cross and left. Amore made himself comfortable in a chair. He was here for the duration. Frankie went about his business. He greeted the hearse driver and issued a few instructions. He opened the lower half of the casket. Jane was wearing socks, but the Magli shoes were missing. *That son of a . . .* , he thought. But he also smiled. He retrieved a metal crank and proceeded to lower the spring mattress. Once the bedding was lowered, he closed the bottom and then the top lid of the casket.

The hearse driver and Frankie rolled the casket out to the lift and into the hearse. Amore, like an honorary pallbearer, was never more than five feet away, never letting the casket out of his sight.

With Frankie in the front seat, the hearse proceeded to church. Three black Lincoln Navigators trailed behind, forming an impressive funeral cortège. Frankie tried to calm himself, rubbing his palms together. His hands were shaking—his knees, too. "Are you okay, Mr. Grace?" the driver asked. Frankie nodded. "I know, he was your friend. Never easy to bury family or friends."

❊ ❊ ❊

Upstairs, Tim and Nino were watching the monitor. "That bastard won't go away. He's onto something," Tim said.

Nino agreed. "Do you have all your papers?" Nino asked. Tim patted his breast jacket. He went to the closet and put on his shoes, the Bruno Magli.

"It's time," he said. Tim took one last look at the office. "Let's go," he said. In a moment, they were in the limo. Tim was pensive. "What time is our flight?" he asked as he jumped into the limousine.

"Four o'clock. We have to be there three hours before. It's international."

Tim nodded. He leaned forward and banged on the glass divider. "Stop, stop the car," he said to the driver.

"What are you doing?" Nino protested.

"I have to make a stop. Take us to St. Catherine's," he ordered.

Nino's eyes bugged out of his head. He couldn't yell. "Are you crazy, *patzo*? What are you doing?"

"Relax, Nino. I can't miss my own funeral. I just can't. I'll never forgive myself."

"Tim, this is crazy—*you* are crazy," he whispered. "You will ruin everything, all the plans, the risk. You can't."

"Nino, I'll be careful. No one will be expecting me. We have time. It's only 11:15."

"No, I insist. I am responsible for you. I promised *zio*."

Tim would not take "No" for an answer. The limo pulled up near the church. "You want me to miss this?" he asked. The hearse was in front of the church. News crews meandered on the sidewalk. Cameras were set up. A team of agents from the FBI were also filming all the comings and goings. Tim could spot them anywhere. A few stragglers hurried into church. Police cars, detectives, and a contingent of crooks and gangsters stood out to him. "Go around back," he directed. The driver obliged. Tim took off his toupee. "Sit tight. I'll be right back."

"*Patzo*," Nino yelled after him. "*Calvo patzo!*"

Tim approached the church, looking for a point of entry. He walked across the grotto. A granite statue of St. Catherine stood guard over a dormant garden. Overgrown brownish weeds had taken the place of begonias and periwinkle in the porcelain pottery. A service entrance led to the basement. Organ music and singing were echoing off the marble floors and throughout the nave. "May the road rise to meet you." He followed the sound, up a rickety wooden staircase, each step squealing beneath his feet. From a side door on the main floor, he peeked inside. *Nice crowd,* he thought, *for a weekday and all.* But the view left him wanting. He inched toward a spiral staircase and followed it up to the choir loft. He was above the crowd now, looking down. He saw the organist and a vocalist ahead of him. It was dark but for a small lamp above the sheet music on the organ. He crawled like a soldier in combat through the choir loft until he reached the front. His bald dome appeared over the rail. He now had a bird's-eye view. Tracy was sitting in the front row. She was in black. *Finally,* Tim thought. She had on a veil and was dabbing her eyes. *Allergies,* he finally concluded. He had to admit, she looked elegant, Jackie O-esque. Next to her was her cousin Bernard—the very one who'd come to his wedding without a gift. *What nerve. Who wears a yarmulke to a Catholic funeral mass?* Bernard was blowing his nose and wiping his eyes. Tim understood cousin Bernard was mourning a loss, namely, a $95,000 investment in a Tim-inspired LLC created to buy delinquent tax liens. Tim had let him in on the ground floor. First stop, basement. Go figure.

Frankie was at the end of the pew, Cardio and Johnny a few rows behind. The crew from Paradise was sitting together and crying. *Geeze, these Costa Ricans are emotional,* Tim thought. At the back of the church, he saw Amore, with a face he'd never forget—made for a funeral. The stiffs with wrinkled suits had to be with him. In one pew were Chinese men under the direction of his friend Wong. Two pews behind them was Sergi and his Albanian crew and would-be tormentors, and across the aisle, was Yakoff and the Russians. Sam Napoli and his crew were there, certainly the best dressed of all the gangs. *What do Russians know from Brioni?* More importantly, Tim knew why they were all there. Even from a distance, he could see the look on their faces—anger. Retribution would not be theirs. They got beat. It wasn't his intention. He got in too deep, in stages, incrementally, first body and then soul.

There were others, too, like old lady Philomena. She owned the coffee shop near Tim's office. She had his coffee and Scratch Off tickets ready every morning. It had been his first stop in the morning for more than 20 years. She was crying. He felt a sudden sadness for having made her cry. He wanted to find a way to let her know, to whisper in her ear not to cry, not to worry, he was okay. In the pews was his dry-cleaner as well, Nicky, who detailed his car, and his buddies from the cigar bar. He had hurt a lot of people by faking his death, and it had only just occurred to him.

Frankie was fidgeting, his knee bouncing up and down. *Understandable,* Tim thought. The men behind him must be somewhat incredulous at what they were witnessing, he was sure. But there it was—his casket, his widow, his friends, a priest, a real funeral. Who could argue? Tim Collins was dead and, with him, his debts. At that moment, as he looked at his casket, he had a profound sense of the tentative nature of life itself.

He looked at the clock over the church doors. Time to go. But then he heard the priest announce a eulogy. He saw Johnny hand Cardio something that he put into his mouth. He watched as Cardio struggled toward the podium. Johnny steadied him down the side aisle as far as he could. He missed one step but caught himself as he approached the microphone. Tim felt a chill. Cardio didn't look well. *This whole thing must have put a strain on him*, he thought.

The hot pepper Cardio had just swallowed kicked in as he approached the podium. His eyes watered, and his voice cracked as he spoke. "To paraphrase Shakespeare," Cardio began, "the bad men do live on after them while the good is interred with their bones. It seems to me that it shouldn't be that way. Maybe it should be opposite." *Nice start*, Tim thought. Cardio continued, "I've known Tim Collins nearly 50 years. Yet, I guess I didn't know him as well as I thought. Then again, who really knows anyone? If you read the papers or watch the news, there's a lot being said about Tim, much conjecture, innuendo. But, should we let that be all that defines him? Shouldn't we let the bad be buried with him and let the good live on?" Tim leaned back and took it all in, hardly recognizing the person Cardio was describing. Cardio hit all the right notes, reminding people of his generosity and willingness to help anyone. He liked the line about being the life of the party, a presence. *Well done, Cardio.* He reminded people of Tim's big, booming laugh. "Yes, Tim Collins was larger than life." Tim took a deep breath. After listening to all the kind words Cardio said about him, he came to the conclusion Cardio was one heck of a liar. He peeked back over the railing. People were crying; some heads were bowed in prayer. He realized there were more prayers than he deserved, more kind words than he'd earned.

"So," Cardio concluded, "whatever we know about him today, whatever news comes out, place it in that box, and burn it with him. Remember instead that smile, that laugh, the double hand-shake, and the hug. Those are the things that should survive him. It's what any of us would want for ourselves. For the good that we do to be remembered. I know I would." *Good point*, Tim thought. After some coughing, Cardio concluded. "Each of us is more than our worst deeds and less than our best. We can only strive to be better with the knowledge that we know not the time or place. I pray that Tim is in a better place. I know he is. He is in the land of the sun, and the land of the sea."

As Cardio left the podium, Frankie motioned the pallbearers forward. As they prepared to proceed out of the church, the vocalist started singing "Danny Boy."

It proved to be too much for Tim. It was overwhelming. There, in the same place he was baptized, confirmed, and promised to love, honor, and obey, the first time, lay his casket. He had come full circle. He had no idea his funeral would have such an effect on him or the many people who were actually crying at his passing. Tim began crying, too. His sobs echoed throughout the choir loft, across the spires. His funeral, from what he could see, was a hit. It had the desired effect. People were actually crying for him. Except for the Russians, the Albanians, the Chinese, Napoli and the Italians, and Amore and the Carabinieri.

Tim wiped his nose on his sleeve. He was a sucker for "Danny Boy." The whole thing was too emotional for him. He was crying at his own funeral. He watched as Frankie led the casket from the altar. Marco jumped out of his pew to escort Tracy. Tim looked at the clock. It was time. He had to go. As he started to leave, he tripped over a pew. The noise echoed throughout the church. Everyone turned their head in his direction. He lay quiet for a second until he heard the priest continue and the music play. Following the same path, he made his way from the church. He moved quickly across the grotto into the waiting limousine.

"You should have been there, Nino. What a beautiful funeral. Frankie did a good job, and you should have heard Cardio's eulogy. Right out of the book of *Bullshitagus*. His delivery could have been better. A lot of words got stuck in his throat. He coughed a lot, like he was choking on something."

"*Patzo*," Nino said. The limousine pulled away slowly. Tim turned to look out the back in time to see his casket being placed in the hearse as Tracy, Frankie, Cardio, Johnny Paradise, Sam Napoli, Reno Amore, Sergi, Wong, and Dimitri looked on. *Funerals*, he noted, *made for strange bedfellows.*

＊　＊　＊

Amore watched the proceedings with great interest. His agents gathered around him. "We are missing something here," he told them. "We are missing something." They watched as Marco escorted Tracy back to the limousine. The hearse pulled away from the church slowly. Behind it were three Lincoln Navigators with the feds, two Cadillac Escalades with Napoli and crew, and three Hyundais loaded with the Chinese. The Albanians and Russians carpooled in a Mercedes SUV. Frankie wasn't expecting this. He had to admit it made for an impressive procession. On his best day, not even Tim could have imagined so many people would want to witness his funeral pyre. He took the scenic route to the cemetery, deciding to make a final pass by the places that were near and dear to Tim. It was a ritual and a good way to kill time and break chops.

Dutifully the cortège followed, making lefts and rights through Inlet Cove, across intersections and under overpasses. He passed the Collins Agency and paused a moment; then he proceeded on, past two cigar bars and a handful of cocktail lounges. Pedestrians paused on the street to tip their hat, wave goodbye, or bow their head. There might have been a middle finger or two as well. Tim would understand.

※

Chapter XXXVIII

As *Nino and Tim pulled up to JFK airport,* a thought came to Tim. "What if this doesn't work?" he asked.

"What do you mean?"

"My identity. What if it doesn't work?"

Nino did not know the answer. He looked at the fake passport and then at Tim. "I don't know, but we are about to find out. Keep that thing off your head until we are inside." He took luggage from the trunk and handed it to Tim. JFK was a madhouse. "Try not to look nervous or out of place."

"Right, easy enough," he said. Inside the airport, he was just another bald head among thousands of travelers. He stopped in the restroom and placed his toupee upon his head.

"Al Italia," Nino said to a porter. "Business Class." The man placed their luggage on a cart and escorted them ahead of the line through security. Tim had his passport in his hand. He was quivering. Nino took it from him and handed it across the counter to an attractive ticket clerk in a pillbox hat.

"Senore Greco?"

Tim was looking around, expecting a hand to grab him at any moment. He didn't recognize his new name. Nino kicked him.

"Yes, Greco, Luciano Greco."

She examined his passport, scanned it, checked boxes, and returned it to him with a boarding pass. "Have a pleasant flight." The porter put the luggage on the conveyor belt.

Nino followed, and, in moments, the two were seated in the complimentary lounge for business-class Al Italia customers. Tim was sweating. He'd passed the first and most important test of all. He was on his way to his new life. They settled back with a glass of Chianti.

"What's the plan, when we get to Italy?" Tim asked.

Nino stretched his legs. "I need to spend time in Rome, perhaps a month or so. I have business meetings and you will be on your own. Try not to get into trouble."

"Trouble? Like how?"

"Like taking stone from the Colosseum for a souvenir. Then we will head toward Sicily by way of the scenic route, over land down the Amalfi Coast through Calabria and eventually ferry over to Palermo. We will take our time and blend into the countryside. You are not in a hurry, are you?"

Tim shrugged. "Me? I have no place I need to be."

Nino called his uncle to report. Johnny understood the message. *The birds are flying today.*

❉

Chapter XXXIX

Back at the restaurant, Johnny relaxed after the phone call. He whispered the message into Cardio's ear. The two toasted. Hungry mourners were arriving. Johnny pulled out all the stops, explaining that Tim would have wanted it that way. Waiters roamed the dining room passing appetizers, meatballs, rollatini, shrimp. Marco was very attentive to Tracy. There was an open bar. Johnny recognized most of the people but not all. He understood that people come out of the woodwork for a good funeral luncheon. Local businessmen, passing acquaintances of Tim, old friends from high school, and even wives number one and two were there. Wife number one was the one with the teacup Shih Tzu. Johnny opened the floor to anyone who might want to say something nice about Tim.

It was a quiet luncheon.

❊

Chapter XL

As the hearse made its way toward the crematory, Frankie was mindful of the procession behind him. He slowed as they entered the gates. The crematory was a gothic structure that sat in the middle of a sprawling cemetery. In the distance, grayish smoke spewed from chimney stacks contrasting against a blue sky, a morbid reminder to Frankie of the tentative nature of life—dust we are. The haze represented all that was left of once-living, breathing bodies, that loved and walked upon the Earth, that laughed and cried and dreamed. All of it now up in smoke and reduced to worthless ash. Frankie often grappled with the futility of it all, of life itself. It was just one of the plausible reasons he offered for his affinity for wine and song.

The hearse driver backed up to large bronze doors. An attendant swung them open and greeted Frankie. "Cold enough for you, Mr. Grace?"

"Sure is," Frankie said. He handed the cremation permit and authorizations to him. Frankie saw Amore and company walking toward him, leading an eclectic group of curious onlookers with a vested interest in the proceedings. After checking the permits, the attendant helped transfer the casket from the hearse onto a truck.

"An oak," he said. "We don't see many wood caskets anymore."

In the anteroom outside the burn room, there were a dozen corrugated boxes, each containing human remains. Names were written on them unceremoniously with magic marker. This was the new face of the funeral business. Naked bodies in cardboard, lined up in an assembly line, for cremation, indistinguishable, one after the other. What was missing was anyone to say goodbye, anyone to place a final flower, say a final prayer. It crystalized how things had changed. As Frankie thought about it, he recognized the irony. Tim was the only one who actually had people who cared enough to see it through to the end, for whatever reason.

The oak casket got star treatment. Tim would like that. The attendant rolled it ahead of the corrugated boxes. "A fine piece of wood," he said. He opened another set of doors. There were eight retorts fired up. Giant oven motors were humming; furnaces were roaring. A blast of hot air hit him. It was hard to hear or think. The smell of burning flesh was inevitable and upsetting. They rolled the casket to the retort. Flames were visible behind a glass peephole on a steel door. The attendant opened it. A burst of heat filled the room. The controlled flame in the retort would reach two thousand degrees. Frankie was about to slide his best friend into the retort. He tried to look sad, reluctant.

"Wait." It was Amore. He was standing by the door, watching every move. He approached Frankie with agents. The other members of the funeral cortège stayed back, content to let the law handle things.

"Open it," Amore ordered.

"Excuse me?" Frankie said.

"You heard me. I said, 'Open it.'"

The attendant chimed in. "I'm sorry, but it's against policy to open a casket . . ."

Amore didn't look at him. He extended his arm toward the attendant. Amore's credentials were right in front of his face. The badge was impressive. "Open it," he said again.

Frankie felt his knees knocking and wondered if Amore could hear them as well. Beads of sweat were forming on his brow. He pulled a small latch on the casket and opened the lid. Amore walked around, never taking his eyes off Frankie, until he was standing by his side. Only then did he look into the casket, only to see Tim Collins. Amore was speechless; he scratched his head and his chin, and he tweaked a hair of his mustache. It was then Frankie noticed Tim's hand. The ambient heat from the retort was beginning to melt the epoxy. The hands were the thinnest mold. Frankie knew the ears would be next, followed by the nose, followed by handcuffs.

"I'm sorry, sir," the attendant spoke up. "I can lose my job. A casket can't be opened once it's in here. It's crematory policy."

Amore stepped back. Frankie closed the lid. He made the sign of the cross as he rolled Jane Doe/Tim Collins into the retort. The steel door slammed shut. Frankie put his hand on the door to say goodbye to his friend for the benefit of all who were looking on. He also took the opportunity to take a deep breath. Everyone watched, seemingly satisfied and beginning to assess their loss. For some, it was money; for others, it was justice. Frankie had to laugh to himself as he watched the jumble of dejected losers walk back to their vehicles. *A funeral is supposed to bring people together. This one certainly did.* A strange assortment of cops and crooks pulled away from the cemetery. *You're a piece of work, Tim Collins. Rest in peace.*

But it wasn't over yet. A second hearse was on the way, carrying another oak casket filled with bones. Frankie cleared the papers again for the remains of Jane Doe, AKA Skully. The casket was the same oak unit. The attendant helped transfer it from the hearse. There was nothing unusual about the weight now that Cardio's debris had been packed into the casket. "You're having a good week," he said. "Two good oaks." Frankie nodded. The attendant was still rambling about the scene earlier. "Who was that guy? What nerve. I could lose my job."

Together, they rolled the casket into the retort. It was done, the plan complete. All the evidence would soon discolor the blue sky. Up in smoke went Jane Doe and Skully. "I'll pick the ashes up tomorrow," Frankie said.

❄   ❄   ❄

Frankie arrived at Paradise Restaurant in time for a series of toasts. Johnny hung his coat. "They're cleared," Johnny reported. "Should be boarding by now. No hiccups."

He took a deep breath. "Can you believe we pulled it off?" Frankie asked.

Johnny laughed. "No, I can't," he said.

Frankie took a seat next to Cardio. "Skully is gone," he said, "along with all your past," he added. He looked at Cardio for a reaction. Cardio digested the comment, nodded, and lifted a glass. His arm seemed to cramp as he attempted a toast. Frankie continued, "There was a little glitch. Amore is a stubborn guy, but we were lucky. I'll explain later."

The two downed a shot. Frankie had a chill in his bones. The booze helped. "Hard to believe," Cardio noted. "This is the first time we are here drinking and eating and Tim's not here."

"Like he said, no one wants to be the guest of honor at a funeral luncheon."

❄

Chapter XLI

At the airport in Rome, Tim followed Nino as he navigated through a maze of organized confusion. Their re-entry was facilitated by Global Entry. "Welcome home, Mr. Greco." Nino kicked him again.

"Oh, thank you. *Gracias.*" Frustrated, Nino just rolled his eyes.

"Now I will show you my country," Nino said. After a few days in Rome, Nino drove down the Amalfi Coast on his way to Naples. The final destination, Sciacca, Sicily. Music blared, and Nino sang along. Tim was critical. "Sounds like you're crying, not singing."

"My friend, these are *canzone Napolitana*. Neapolitan music," he explained, "always involves crying. Either the singer's mother has died, or their girlfriend has died, or their wife has died, or their wife *and* mother have died. In any case, they are always crying." The music, if not the ride down the narrow mountain, was bearable. The road down the Amalfi coast was better suited for a bicycle lane. Nino was expertly maneuvering around tour buses at the slightest opportunity. A wrong move would send them flying toward their certain death. *That would be the very definition of irony*, Tim thought. "Sit back, my friend. Listen, and enjoy my country," Nino suggested as he sang along with the car radio. "This is Claudio Villa, one of my favorites."

Later, having safely arrived in Positano, Tim and Nino sat barefoot on the terrace of Le Sirenuse, sipping a Negroni and staring out over the Gulf of Naples.

Tim absorbed the horizon. Positano sprawled vertically beneath and above him. Time stood still. Sunlight sparkled off the golden mosaic dome of Chiesa St. Assunta. From the summit of Montepertuso to the hamlet of Nocelle, a fusion of colors stippled the vista. The Mediterranean sun sat like a shiny dime pinned against the sky. Its rays danced off silver and beige pebbles on the Spiaggia Grande. Homes built into the mountain's face glimmered like gems, smiling back at the sea and boasting a spectrum of a thousand tints of color, like giant Crayola Crayons, lined up one upon the other: whites, pinks, and blues returning the sun's rays to a blue sky over a *mare piu blu*. Tim took a deep breath, as if to swallow it all in. "This must be the most beautiful property on Earth," he said. In the distance, a mandolin mourned, echoing down cobblestone paths and terrazzo walls. "I think someone's mother has died," Tim reported.

※

Chapter XLII

Back in the states, the following afternoon, Frankie retrieved two boxes containing the cremated remains. They were returned in nondescript plastic containers, each labeled, named, coded, and dated. Inside of each were the pulverized remains of Jane Doe and Skully. Back in his office, Frankie switched the names and identification on each box. Jane Doe's ashes were now Jane Doe's ashes. Tim Collins ashes were Skully's. As it turned out, Jane Doe had a name. She was missing from her group home. They notified the police and identified her. Jane Doe was Mathilda Todd.

"How she wound up dead at a bus stop with a small valise and no identification is still a mystery," Gregoria said. In the meantime, I faxed you the information we have."

Frankie adjusted the death certificate, and, out of a sense of guilt or appreciation, he placed her remains in a classic pewter urn and had her name engraved on it. A few days later, he purchased a niche at the cemetery and brought her to be interred. Mathilda had walked upon the Earth. She lived, loved, and died—and saved his friend's life in the process. Now there was a plaque with her name to mark her presence. He placed a small bouquet and said, "Thank you." She did not die in vain. This permanent memorial was her reward. At least some of the blanks had been filled in. As for Skully, AKA Tim Collins, he had to think.

He sat at his desk, pondering all that had transpired and tried to think about what still may. He felt uncomfortable having the ashes that were supposed to be those of Tim Collins. He did not know why, but his instincts gnawed at him. He opened his desk drawer and saw Tim's phone. He picked it up, sat back, and looked at it. He remembered when he'd stuffed it in his drawer. He toyed with the phone, from one hand to the other, deep in thought. He powered the phone on and heard the ring tone, "Fly Me to the Moon." A smile came across his face. A solution had revealed itself. He had an idea.

Weeks passed without incident. Frankie flew down to Florida but was too antsy to relax, so he returned after a week. All was quiet on all fronts—too quiet. A fatalist at heart, Frankie was nervous. He went for lunch as usual and ate alone at the bar. Johnny went about his business. Cardio missed a few lunches, and Frankie thought nothing of it. *Maybe better not to be seen together for a while. What we did couldn't be that easy to get away with.* So, he ate and drank and waited, waited for some repercussions.

Johnny was receiving cryptic messages from Nino. They began and ended with "This guy is *patzo!*"

❋

Chapter XLIII

*R*eno Amore was one unhappy federal agent. He had an uneasy feeling in the pit of his stomach that antacids didn't cure. He'd missed something, and it bedeviled him. He hated being outsmarted, played. He looked at the file over and over, the photographs and the connections. *What did I miss?* he wondered. Adding to his anger was the late delivery of a report from FBI Headquarters in Manhattan. The file from the agents watching don Eddie Fontana landed on his desk. It had been lost in a bureaucratic shuffle. He studied the report and the accompanying photographs. It chronicled the visitors to Ciao Mein Restaurant. There, on two occasions, were Frankie Grace and the late Tim Collins. He pulled on the short hairs of his mustache as he tried to make the connection. What did they have to do with don Fontana? What was Grace carrying when he left? One thing he knew for sure: The investigation wasn't over.

He requested archived FBI files. He confirmed that Frankie Grace was the son-in-law of John Ballsziti, head of the Ballsziti crime family. Ballsziti ran operations on the east coast until his arrest in '84. He died in prison. Frankie's file showed he was an ancillary player, with no criminal involvement. He seemed to be more of a victim of circumstance. He read the file on Johnny Paradise, his father, and the connection with Sam Napoli.

"What about this Dr. Odelli?" he asked his investigators. "If this was a scam, why would a professional, a doctor, be involved? I want to know more about him."

※

Chapter XLIV

A few weeks later, Officer Hopper was called into a meeting at the FBI field office in White Plains. He was told there were questions he needed to answer regarding the night Tim Collins died. He brought his notebook and hoped to make a good impression. He dusted his patent-leather shoes and showed up in uniform. He fidgeted with his fingers and patted down his hair as he waited in an outer office.

The relentless Amore sat at the head of a conference table with a stenographer and two other obscure agents at his side. "Officer Hopper, you know why you're here?"

"Yes, sir. I was informed," Hopper answered.

"The evening of February 15, you responded to a call that reported a death at 411 Cove Avenue. The Collins Agency, I believe."

Hooper thought for a moment. "Yes, yes I did."

"Tell us, what did you do? What did you observe?"

Hopper was slow and deliberate as he recalled the events of that evening. They were indelibly etched in his brain, a night he would never forget. For absolute accuracy, he referred to a clumpy black pad that he carried with him. "I responded," he began, "to a call from my desk sergeant. There was a report of a death. He gave me the address." Hopper flipped through the pages. "I arrived at circa 9:30 p.m." In Hopper's mind, case closed.

"Go on," Amore urged.

"On the scene was a Mr. Frank Grace. He introduced himself as a friend of the deceased. He'd discovered the body."

"Did you see the body?"

Hopper's mouth went dry. His tongue got caught in his lips. The very question made him think that maybe, just maybe, he should have. Now he weighed his words carefully. He sensed danger should a word be misspoken and also wanted to add an air of profession-alism to his report. This could be a career move. "I saw a body. It was on the floor behind the desk. Mr. Grace explained that it was his friend," he looked down at his notes, "one Timothy Collins, the now-mentioned deceased." He looked at his pad again and read. "Mr. Grace stated he was to meet the aforementioned Mr. Collins for dinner, but the aforementioned Mr. Collins did not respond to repeated calls from the before-mentioned Mr. Grace. The before-mentioned Mr. Grace proceeded to the address prementioned to find the aforementioned Mr. Collins in a state of not being alive anymore." *That went well*, he thought.

Amore reached for a packet of aspirin in his pocket. He tore it open and swallowed two pills without water.

"Did you know Mr. Grace was also an undertaker as well as a dinner date?"

"I didn't think anything . . ."

"Did you recognize Mr. Collins?" Amore asked.

"The aforementioned?"

"Yes, the aforementioned Mr. Collins."

Hopper fidgeted in his seat. He couldn't get comfortable. "Well, inasmuch as it was dark, and I did not personally know previously the aforementioned Mr. Collins, I assumed. . . ." There—the dreaded "assumed" word had come out of him, much to his dismay. "I figured," not much better, "that it was the aforementioned Mr. Collins, whose body I saw from a distance and whom was reported to be Mr. Collins by the before-mentioned Mr. Grace."

Amore was scratching his head in frustration. "Did you, or did you not see the dead body of Tim Collins lying on the floor behind his desk on the night of February 12, 2018?"

Hopper thought for a moment, "No, sir."

"No?" Amore shouted.

"No, sir. It was February 15, I believe."

Amore wiped his brow. "Was he Tim Collins?"

"Who?" Hopper asked. He jumped out of his seat when Amore slammed his hand down on the table.

"Collins, Timothy Collins. Did you or did you not see his dead body?"

Hopper's black notebook fell to the floor. He inched it close with his foot and reached for it. "I don't know Mr. Collins, the aforementioned deceased, personally. I wouldn't know if it was him or not, the aforementioned." He looked down like an embarrassed schoolboy. Then, thinking it might help, he said, "I did smell him, though."

"You smelled him?" Amore repeated.

"Yes, sir. I wrote it down. There was a terrible stench from the body. The office was steamy hot. I remember. I wrote it down. It was a nauseating smell. Mr. Grace showed me the thermostat."

"He did, did he? Other than the smell, did you identify the body as Timothy Collins?"

"Again sir, I didn't know Mr. Collins. I only assumed, figured, thought." Hopper's eyes opened wide. "But, Mr. Grace gave me Mr. Collins's watch for safekeeping. It was engraved with his name."

"A watch?" Amore sounded interested in this development.

"Yes, sir. I examined it. It was engraved with the deceased's name. I placed it in a pouch and turned it into my captain for safekeeping. It's in the safe at the station. I followed proper chain of custody." He smiled.

"What happened next?"

"Uh," looking at his notes, "a Dr. Odelli arrived. He walked over to the now-deceased and felt for a pulse, I assumed, figured."

"Was there anything unusual between them?"

"Can you explain the question?"

Amore spoke slowly, allowing each word to fall clearly from his lips. "Was there anything odd or unusual about the interaction between the doctor and Mr. Grace?"

Hopper looked to his pad for answers. He shook his head. "No, no. It all seemed very professional. I heard the doctor on the phone with the medical examiner. Mr. Grace was pacing back and forth. Then the doctor hung up and told Mr. Grace that the medical examiner saw no need for an autopsy. He was clear to remove the body."

"Did you help him? Did you see the body up close?"

Hopper recalled it was about that time that his gastric juices regurgitated in his stomach. "Well," he said, "no."

"So, if I understand you correctly, which is not easy, you never saw the body of Mr. Collins. For all you know, it could have been anybody."

Hopper's head tilted like a curious puppy. "At that hour of the night? I'm called by my dispatcher to go to the Collins Agency. I'm told that a Mr. Collins is dead and a Mr. Grace is there. I had no reason not to think it wasn't who they said it was. Was it?"

"Did you help Mr. Grace remove the body?"

"Uh, I, I was going to, I was about to. I would have, but Mr. Grace said he had to get a spray because there were maggots on the body."

"Maggots?"

Hopper nodded.

"Officer Hopper, do you know how long it takes for maggots to show up on a dead body?"

"No," Hopper admitted.

Amore calmly closed the file and pulled on his mustache. His mustache twitched. "You can go."

Hopper rose from his seat. "Agent Amore, may I ask one question?"

"What is it?"

"I was hoping to join the FBI and have an application pending at Quantico. Would I be able to use your name as a reference?"

Amore came from behind the table. "I'll save you the trouble. I'll call them for you."

Hopper was elated. "Thank you so much. Thank you."

Amore turned to his agents. "Something smells here, and it's not only the body that was in that office. And why would Collins smell so bad? He wasn't dead that long. Why would there be maggots?"

His agents all nodded in agreement and took notes.

❋

Chapter XLV

It was mid-April when Reno Amore arrived at Tim's home with a warrant. He handed it to Tracy, who opened the door. "What now?" she asked. "I thought this was over." There was luggage in the foyer.

"You're planning a trip?"

"Yes," she said, "if it's any of your business. I'm going on a trip to South America."

Amore filed that information in his brain. He explained that they would be going through the house. "Have at it," she said. "Let me know if you find anything of value. He certainly didn't leave it to me. He left me in a mess, bills up my ass, and not a dime in savings." She omitted the pending insurance settlement.

Amore's agents went through the house. He looked around as well. In the master bedroom, there were five Styrofoam heads on a bureau. There was a toupee on three of the five heads. He looked at Tracy, who was on his heels. "What is it?" she asked.

"Your husband had five toupees?" he asked.

She nodded. "Of course. He changed on and off, so they'd be fresh. He was vain, in case you didn't know."

"There seems to be one missing, then. He had one during the wake, and there are three here. There seems to be one missing."

202

"Maybe at his barber," she suggested. "He rotated them, so they'd be shampooed and blown out regularly."

Amore nodded. "Mrs. Collins, where are your husband's ashes? That's what we are looking for."

She was puzzled. "His ashes? I don't know. I haven't gotten around to it. What would I even do with them? Anyway, if that's why you're here, you're wasting your time. I did not get his ashes back."

Amore believed her. It made sense. He recalled the investigators, and they left the premises. "One more question, Mrs. Collins. Who was your husband's barber?" he asked.

※

Chapter XLVI

R*eviewing this case from top to bottom* was time consuming. Amore was following every lead, old and new, and looking at them from different angles. He paused at one in particular. "You see this midget with the tall blonde?' he asked his aide. "I want to know who he is." He even interviewed Tim's barber. The missing toupee was bothering him. The barber confirmed that he serviced Tim's toupee but wasn't currently working on one. Amore was ready to confront Frankie Grace with the evidence. His gut told him he had been scammed, but that contradicted what his own eyes had witnessed at the crematory. It was all too neatly packaged for his taste. He did not believe in coincidence, and the death of Tim Collins fell into that category. If, somehow, someway, Collins had pulled this off, he would have had to leave the country. He remembered Tracy saying she was going on a trip. Following his gut, Amore contacted Interpol. Maybe, just maybe, Mrs. Collins was going to South America to meet her husband. Maybe she was part of the scam. Amore didn't think Collins was smart enough to pull this off alone. He had to have help—friends close enough to risk everything. Amore pressed his investigators for more information on Frankie Grace and Dr. Claudio Odelli. Frankie was easy. The

FBI had a jacket on him that went back 40 years but ended there, too. He was son-in-law to the infamous don John Ballsziti, now deceased. Amore concluded that Grace had the street smarts to pull something like this off. His association with the other candy-store gangster, Johnny Paradise, made that more likely. But the doctor puzzled him. How did they get Dr. Odelli involved? He was a man with so much to lose. Why would he join this conspiracy? He leaned back in his chair and stroked his mustache, which was showing signs of thinning.

※

Chapter XLVII

Weeks turned into months, passing without incident. Frankie knew it was a false calm. He knew Amore had him in his sights. It was a waiting game. He couldn't let his guard down. There was one piece of good news. It was hidden on page 32 of the *New York Post*. "The charges against reputed don Eddie Fontana were tossed out." It seemed from the article that, among the unintelligible words the don uttered on the day of his arrest was the name of his lawyer, Sun Woo Yoo. Thinking it was gibberish, the feds did not call Mr. Yoo, which violated Mr. Fontana's right to counsel. Frankie laughed. A Mandarin lawyer, of course—classic Eddie. There was also a check in the mail from Tim's lawyer for funeral expenses. It did not cover expenses, but his heart was in the right place.

✳

Chapter XLVIII

At a morning meeting of his investigators, someone reported, "The little man in the photo is an old-timer from the Bronx. An embalmer, also known as The Fixer because of his expertise in reconstruction." Amore was then handed a report on Dr. Claudio Odelli. The agent reported, "He's clean. He went to Johns Hopkins and graduated in 1978. He did a two-year residency at the Mayo Clinic in Phoenix. Then he came east and took a position at United Hospital in Chester, New York. He stayed there for three years and went into private practice *circa* 1984. United Hospital has since closed its doors. His jacket is clean—no lawsuits, no malpractice claims, stellar reputation with patients, and countless peer reviews."

Amore's mustache twitched. "Did you say Johns Hopkins?" The words clicked something in his brain. He relived each interaction he'd had with Odelli—at the hospital, the funeral home, the doctor's office. He remembered the night in the emergency room. He and a bevy of agents had been adding to the organized confusion. Amore watched and listened. He cornered Frankie for questions. He tried to speak with Odelli as well, but the doctor brushed him off. "Not now," he'd said. Then it hit him.

He recalled Collins yelling from his hospital bed, fighting with Odelli about not wanting to be admitted.

Amore reprised the whole scene vividly. He also recalled waiting in Odelli's office the next day. He made himself comfortable waiting for the doctor to arrive. He looked around the office. He remembered the very place where Odelli's license, certificates, and accreditations were hanging on the wall. He saw it clear as day in his mind's eye. Graduate of Johns Hopkins School of Medicine alongside a diploma from St. George's School of Medicine. There was also certificate of residency from the Mayo Clinic in Arizona and a medical license.

As he thought about it now, it didn't add up. Collins, Odelli, Paradise, Grace. *Who are these people?* he wondered. He was determined to find out.

Interpol relayed information from St. George University in Grenada. There had been a Claudio Odelli in attendance. He graduated with honors in 1980. "By the way," the investigator added, "he never took his USMLT." That was met with silence. "The United States Medical Licensing Test," he explained. "As far as we can see, he's not certified. He never had a license to practice medicine."

But investigators at the field office in Arizona confirmed that there was also a Dr. Claudio Odelli on staff at the Mayo Clinic. He later went into private practice, until his death in 1980. The agents retrieved an obituary from the archive of the *Arizona Republic News*.

"Odelli, Claudio Dr., of Phoenix, died peacefully on May 11, 1980. He was 92. Dr. Odelli was a physician at the Mayo Clinic before going into private practice. He is predeceased by his wife Antoinette and brother Sebastiano. He is survived by his nephew, Claudio Odelli of New York. Services were private."

The next stop for Amore was an interview with the former administrator of United Hospital, Josh Lang. The hospital had gone bankrupt in 1990. Amore arranged a meeting and told him who he was interested in. The administrator was glad to oblige but needed time to pull whatever information was available on Dr. Claudio Odelli.

"I remember him well," the administrator said as they sat over a cup of coffee. "Odelli was a master diagnostician. He lectured and was well respected by his peers. He was a benevolent man. Generous with his time. He volunteered at the free clinic three times a week. Still does, from what I know." He passed a file across the table. "These are copies of what we had. Since the hospital closed, all records were scanned. It wasn't easy to track this down. What's this about?"

Amore flipped through the file. "There's one little thing that bothers me," he said. Lang buttered a muffin. "The Dr. Odelli you know, the one who graduated Hopkins and worked at the Mayo Clinic before coming to you. The one who lectured and all."

"Yes," Lang said.

"He would have been 140 years old. How would you explain that?"

Coffee sprayed from his lips. He gagged on the muffin. He stuttered, "Why, well . . ." He took the file back to examine it. "I can't say. You must be mistaken. We wrote to Mayo for references. They're all here. He had his degree and license number. It all checked out. I assure you. You must be mistaken."

"I'm afraid not."

Lang kept looking through the files. "Are these forgeries? Is that what you're saying? Is he a fraud?"

"That's what I'm saying. Your Dr. Odelli assumed his uncle's identity. He never went to Johns Hopkins, never did a residency at The Mayo Clinic. He never passed the licensing exam." He slid a copy of Dr. Claudio Odelli's obituary across the table.

Lang was red. "You've got to understand, this was the eighties. Our emergency room was standing-room-only. We were short-handed and happy to have the young doctor join us. I don't understand. We did due diligence."

"It's pretty simple. The man you hired was not a doctor. He was, however, a damn good con artist."

"But how . . . .?"

"I guess, if you wear a bowtie, you can fool a lot of people."

Amore's sixth sense was piecing together the scheme. He did not have all the answers, but now he had enough to squeeze Odelli.

"What happens now?" Lang asked. "Are you arresting him? Do you know the legal implications this will have, the lawsuits?"

"Identity theft is the least of the good doctor's problems," Amore said. With what he now knew, Odelli would be facing disgrace, disrepute, and 30 years of malpractice suits, which he would fight while sitting in a prison. He would break. He was the weak link. Amore smiled. Lang did not, as he thought about the legal repercussions. Amore left him at the table frozen in place. He left him with the check as well.

Armed with this information and the news from the lab at Quantico regarding DNA, Amore was ready to make his move. This troupe of clowns, frauds, thieves, and gangsters would not outsmart him.

※

Chapter XLIX

Frankie's sense of impending doom turned out to be correct. As he sat behind his desk, he saw cars coming into the parking lot and recognized them immediately. It was Reno and company. By this time, Reno knew his way around the funeral home. He watched him enter, cross the lobby, and walk up the spiral staircase to his office. The door was open.

"Mr. Amore, what can I do for you this lovely day?"

Amore was not equally cordial. He walked to a chair across from Frankie and made himself comfortable. He held a thick file and placed it on his lap.

"Mr. Grace, I have some questions for you." Frankie leaned back in his swivel chair.

"Questions? About?"

"General questions, life, death."

"I'm your man, I guess. Do you want to make pre-arrangements?"

"You mean like Tim Collins did, way back in 2015?"

Frank nodded, "Yes, I think it was in '15. I'll have to check. It was around the time of his heart issues."

"Right, right—I've got that," Reno said, fingering through the file. "I imagine he requested to be cremated."

"Obviously," Frankie said. "I wouldn't have done it otherwise."

"Mr. Grace, I spoke with officer Hopper. He was the officer on duty when the death was reported."

"Hopper? If you say so. I don't recall."

"Yes, it was Hopper. He reported a stench. I assume from decomposition of the body. Collins was seen Thursday afternoon at one of his favorite haunts around three in the afternoon, and you called in his death at about 9 p.m. That leaves less than six hours. In your experience, would a body begin to decay in that short time?"

Frankie didn't notice his fingers tapping on the chair. "Stench," he asked. "I don't recall anything unusual, but, then again, my nose has adapted over a lifetime in this business. I will say, it was crazy hot in that office. The thermostat was set to 90+, and heat can accelerate decomposition."

Reno did not take his eyes off Frankie. "And maggots. Is it common for maggots to show up so soon after death?"

"Maggots? I don't recall maggots."

"So, was officer Hopper wrong? He reported that you said there were maggots."

"Hopper? Oh, the officer on the scene. I don't know what he reported. I don't remember maggots. He must be mistaken. I remember him running to the bathroom. It wasn't pretty."

"Mr. Grace, can you tell me about Eddie Fontana?"

"Eddie?"

"Fon-tan-a," he said.

"It doesn't ring a bell," Frankie said.

Reno tossed a photograph across the desk and then another one. Clearly visible were he and Tim on Mulberry Street exiting Ciao Mein Restaurant. "Oh, cousin Eddie, Special Ed. Yes, I know him. Actually, I grew up with him. My parents took him in. They owned a small storefront funeral home." He pointed to photographs on the wall. "I hadn't seen him in years until Tim and I went to Little Italy. Tim was fascinated with my old neighborhood, and, while there, I took a chance to see if Eddie was still around or even alive. It was a good visit. Brought back a lot of memories."

"And on a second trip down memory lane, you left with a pouch of some kind." Reno pointed to the photograph.

Frankie stared at the photograph. A bead of sweat formed on his brow. His mind was racing. If Ciao Mein was under surveillance, what else did Amore know? Was the restaurant bugged? Did they record the conversation? How would he explain the pouch?

"Takeout menus," he said, but it sounded more like a question.

"One more question, Mr. Grace." He produced a photograph of The Chef leaving the funeral home. "You know this man? They call him 'The Fixer' because of his expertise with dead bodies."

Frankie swallowed. "Yes, he's a old friend of my father."

"And it seems he knew Tim Collins, too. Mr. Grace, I won't take up much more of your time." Amore rose from his seat and produced a piece of paper from his pocket. "I have here a warrant for the cremated remains of Timothy Collins."

Frankie's eyes opened wide. "You want Tim's remains?"

"You know, Mr. Grace, science and technology are wonderful things. Such advances. Did you know that, with advances in forensic science, it is now possible to retrieve DNA from cremated remains? It seems that residue remnants of teeth and bone still hold traces of one's DNA even after cremation. We've come a long way. Wouldn't you agree?"

Frankie stopped rocking in his chair. This was a chess match, and he was contemplating his next move. He froze under Amore's gaze.

Frankie rose and walked to the window. "You want Tim's ashes?" he asked again. He pointed to the sky. Then he went to the file cabinet.

He pulled out Tim's file and looked through it. He took out an official document that read, "Certificate of Lunar Burial." "I wish you had asked me a week ago." He read from the document. "This is to certify that on April 8, 2018, the cremated remains of Timothy Collins were expelled from a Moonex Rocket under the direction of Celestis Space Burial. His remains entered the moon's exosphere on a lunar lander and impacted the moon's surface at Mare Tranquilitatis. There they will remain for all eternity." He handed the certificate to Amore.

Amore's jaw remained open as he looked at the document. "Those were his wishes," Frankie said, pointing to the pre-arrangement forms. He offered Tim's file, pointing to the written request. "Fly Me to the Moon," Frankie said. "You know, it was his favorite song." He handed Amore a CD. "Celestis Space Burials arranged the whole thing. They've even memorialized it. You can watch the video. It was all included." He looked out the window. "Quite a tribute, I'd say. We flew him to the moon. Isn't science incredible?"

* * *

Incensed and speechless, Amore stormed out of the office. He had one more opportunity to break up this cabal. That would be with the good Dr. Odelli. Faced with the information he had, Odelli would fold. No sooner did he reach his car than his cell phone vibrated. "Yes," he shouted. "Where? I'm on the way."

* * *

Frankie collapsed in his chair and reached for a bottle of cognac. He deserved it; he needed it. His cell phone pinged. "Frankie?" a voice asked when he answered.

"Yes. Johnny? You won't believe who just left."

"Frankie . . ."

"It was Amore. He wanted Tim's . . ."

"Frankie."

". . . ashes. I had to break the news."

"Frankie!" Johnny shouted. "Frankie, you have to get over here. You have to come to Cardio's place. Frankie, hurry. It's not good."

Frankie pulled up to Cardio's apartment building. There were police cars and a van from the medical examiner's office. Not waiting for an elevator, he bounded up the three flights. On the landing, a cadre of police were outside Cardio's door. Two morgue attendants were waiting with a gurney. He brushed past them. Johnny was sitting at the kitchen table, his head in his hands. He looked up. Frankie recognized the look in his eyes. He had seen it a thousand times over his life—it came with the territory, a job hazard. It was the last look he'd recall before closing his eyes at night, the look that haunted his dreams, the look that roused him from sleep, the look of countless mourners, unabashed, pure, primal grief. Johnny pointed to a back room. Frankie rushed in that direction. Officials were lurking about—shadowy figures, no form or substance. A police officer moved away from the bed. Frankie saw Cardio, fully dressed, bowtie and all, but motionless, frozen in time, dead. On a nightstand, there were a myriad of pill bottles, empty. An array of Ace bandages and leg braces lay atop a nearby chair. A note, handwritten on a yellow legal pad, was clutched in his hands, neatly folded upon his chest.

Frankie's hands held his head steady. His vision blurred. He held onto the door as his legs buckled. A force beyond his control moved him forward—fighting another force, equally determined that he not arrive. At the bedside, Frankie fell to his knees.

Johnny heard plaintive screams billowing from the bedroom throughout the apartment, reverberating through the floorboards to his bones, down the halls, through the building. He broke down in tears, helpless to help either of his friends.

·※·

Chapter L

In Italy, Nino and Tim strolled the Lungo Mare and stopped for espresso. "Nino, do you think I'm a terrible person? Don't answer that. I know the answer. I'm a despicable person. I haven't done a thing right in my whole, worthless life."

Nino thought for a moment. "You must have done something right. You made some very good friends along the way."

Tim shrugged. "That I did," he said. "That I did."

"Anyway, we eat soon," Nino said. "In Italy, it is custom, a *siesta*. Our big meal is in the afternoon. All shops close for hours."

"What's the big deal? We do the same thing at home," Tim observed. "A big meal in the afternoon? Where shall we go? Is there a Four Seasons?"

"Come. You will meet my friends as well."

Nino's position as director of the Eremo in Sciacca gave him entrée to the finest hotels. From the Four Seasons in Florence, to the Santa Caterina in Amalfi, he was a local celebrity everywhere he went. But he also knew the small *trattorias*, the mom-and-pops where one experienced the true flavor of his country.

Nino drove up a winding mountain road and into a petrol station. Original diesel gas pumps were rusting in the gravel yard. A vintage Coke machine guarded the entrance. "We will eat here," he said.

Tim was confused. "This isn't the Four Seasons. It's a friggin' gas station."

"No, no my friend. You must eat at the smallest *trattoria*." He followed as Nino walked beyond the diesel pumps into the small deli featuring panini sandwiches, espresso, and Chinotti beverages. "Sandwiches?" Tim asked.

"Just follow me," Nino said. Tim walked through and toward the back, following an obscure sign, *Il Cortile*. Beyond the door, a panoramic vista sprawled before his eyes, magnificent in its simplicity. Potted plants sat on ancient stone walls, overlooking a cliff. Olive groves and lush greenery danced beneath nature's breath toward an endless canvas of blue horizon. Flowers soaking up the Mediterranean sun were hanging from a trellis that played hide-and-seek with light and shade. Lemon trees encased the courtyard. Their scent infused the air with a fragrant bouquet, almost palatable. A crispness filled his lungs. Tim, never a keen observer of nature, was impressed. The setting took his breath away.

"It's like the friggin' Garden of Eden," he eloquently observed.

Nino nodded in agreement. "This is where the locals eat," Nino explained.

A group of men sat at a long table covered in a white linen cloth. An elegant, elderly woman, with silver hair beautifully layered above her head, greeted him, "*Caro* Nino," she said, planting a kiss on each cheek. She was wearing a pastel-blue evening gown with sequins, covered with a chef's apron. *Strange combination*, Tim thought, *but hey*. There were shouts as Nino approached. "Nino, Nino!" Then the hugging ritual began. After making the rounds, Nino introduced Tim. "This is my friend, Luciano." That called for another round of hugging. Tim was subjected to a dozen bear hugs. He was *"amici," "compare," "fratello."* In no time at all, he was seated, as copious amounts of food were passed toward him. One man poured him wine.

"Vino di castelli—you like?" the man asked.

"How do you say 'Duh' in Italian?" It lost something in translation. In any case, the feast began.

Nino whispered in his ear. "These men are movers and shakers. You see that man, Angelo? He is the olive-oil king of Italy."

Tim was dipping bread in the liquid gold as Nino spoke. "Really," he said. "So, he produces olive oil?"

Nino looked at him. "No, of course not. He imports inferior olive oil from Greece and Africa. Then he changes the label and exports it as a product of Italy, 100 percent virgin. Made a fortune."

"Industrious," he said, choking on the bread.

"No, don't worry. This is the real thing." After a glass of wine, or three, Tim felt right at home. Nino described all his friends, including Sebastiano Paradiso, the head of the local Camorra. "They make the mafia look like altar boys," he explained.

"Any relation?"

"A distant cousin," Nino answered. "I'll introduce you later. Be respectful. You never know when you might need him."

Tim looked at Nino. "Are you kidding? I've kissed more rings than all the Cardinals in Rome."

Nino continued. "And, right across from him is Carlo Faga, a world-renowned designer. Actually, he steals the latest designs from the best houses in Paris and reproduces them for worldwide distribution."

"Knockoffs?"

"Shush, not so loud," Nino whispered. The appetizers kept coming out of the kitchen, one after another, under the watchful eye of *Contessa*. Fish, whiting, clams, crab, lobster. "From the sea to your dish," Nino said. Tim was getting into it. He was laughing as if he understood what was being said. He took prompts from facial expressions, laughed when they laughed, nodded when they nodded. Contessa inspected each dish brought to the table. Like a mother happy to see her children eating, she circled the table, ready to respond to the potential of an empty dish or an empty bottle of wine. "*Mangia, mangia,*" she said. Her smile lit her face. A gold tooth reflected the sun.

"That's Contessa. She is the owner and cook as well," Nino explained.

"I don't know if I can eat more," Tim said.

"Pace yourself. I warn you. You must not insult her. Eat!"

He did. His glass was never empty—nor his dish. Glasses clinked with toast after toast. Silverware rattled, conversations got louder, arms gesticulated. The sunset was stunning. Contessa stood above him, intrigued by the stranger in her midst. But he was with the right people, which made him a welcome guest. She whispered in Nino's ear.

"Order something special," Nino said. "She wants to cook for you."

"I don't know if I can eat more."

She sensed the meaning of his words. She frowned. "You no like?"

"Don't insult her," Nino whispered.

"No, no, I don't want to." Then to Nino, he asked, "Is there a menu?"

Nino's eyes bugged out of his head. Menu was a four-letter word. "Of course not. Just tell her what you want," he begged. Their conversation got the attention of others.

Tim thought for a moment. "Veal parmigiana," he said. He noticed a sudden chill. The terrace fell silent. Other diners stopped mid-fork. Contessa lost all expression, her brows crossed; her gold tooth disappeared behind pursed lips. Wine glasses were frozen mid-sip; forks and knives set down. All banter stopped as all eyes were pointed in his direction. He was embarrassed but didn't know why. "What happened?" he whispered to Nino. "Did the Pope die?"

Nino whispered in his ear, "Costoletto Parmigiana does not exist in Italy. We would never put cheese on a veal cutlet. Only Americans do that, tourist. It's an abomination."

"What should I do?" he asked under his breath.

"Order *porkette*. Say '*porkette*.'"

"*Porkette*," Tim announced.

There was a collective sigh. Slowly conversations began again, glasses were filled, and the gold tooth shone again. "*Chin chin, salute, cent'anni.*" After two more hours of gastronomical indulgence that would make ancient Romans envious, came the *torts*, the *gelato*, the cheesecake, *tortoni, sfoigliatelle* and *cannoli*. *Maginettes* of espresso were brought to the table, along with bottles of *sambuca, anizette,* and *grappa*. Tim looked around the table. He was in a parallel universe. He was thousands of miles from Inlet Cove. Or was he? Tim became quiet as he surveyed the crew around the table.

It could well have been Johnny, Cardio, and Frankie sitting across from him, scooping plates clean with bread, attacking a steak bone for the last edible piece of meat, calling for more wine.

"What are you thinking, my friend?" Nino asked.

"I think the Romeo Club has many affiliates," he observed. "Do they meet every day?"

Nino smiled. "Every day," he answered.

"I could get used to this, very easily." Tim thought of himself as a quick study. He learned *corti* meant a single espresso, and *doppia* meant a double. With an air of pride and a degree of comfort with his new friends, he spoke up. "*Cappuccino.*"

A pall once again descended on the gathering. All conversation stopped; all eyes looked at him. "What did I do now?" he asked.

Nino leaned in and whispered in his ear. "*Cappuccino* only at breakfast. Only in the morning."

"*Doppia,*" the quick study said.

After a receiving line of hugs and kisses, Tim was exhausted. His arm muscles ached. As he walked from the terrace, Contessa stood in the doorway. "*Tutto buono?*" she asked.

Nino came to the rescue. "She wants to know if you enjoyed everything."

"Ah, delicious, *delizioso, delizioso.*" A large smile came over her. She beamed. He smiled, too—happy he'd made her happy. He got daring. "Your dress is beautiful. How do you say, *vestito e bellisima,* beautiful?" He pointed.

She blushed; her eyes twinkled, her tooth, too. "Ah, *questo?*" she said. "Grazie. It's Dior!"

Right.

⁕

Chapter LI

*B*efore *Nino and Tim had left New York,* Johnny had advised his nephew to be careful about communication. "Assume every phone is tapped," he said. So, Nino knew there was something urgent when he saw a call coming in from his uncle. He heard his uncle's voice crack as he explained. Nino fought his own tears upon hearing the news; a chill went through him.

"I have to tell him," Johnny explained.

"No, *zio.* I will. I will find the right time to let him know. It will be better."

"Are you sure?" Johnny asked.

"I think so. I think I should—at the right time, the right place."

They made their way through Amalfi, Salerno, and Calabria. Tim was introduced to Nino's network of friends and associates at each stop. There was no shortage of food and wine. Every day was a feast. He was treated like family.

A week after receiving the news, Nino watched Tim walking along the beach from the hotel balcony in Taormina. Tim stopped and stared out at the sea. His body language, his hunched shoulders, his hands clasped behind his back revealed all that Nino needed to know. It wasn't hard to assume what his friend was thinking. It was the stuff of countless Neapolitan songs: the melancholy of loss and the longing to be back home, with those you love. It was time. He had to break the news. This would not be easy.

Nino walked down to the beach, bringing a dish of olives, glasses, and a bottle of white wine under his arm. They sat together, just beyond the reach of methodical waves encroaching ever closer.

"How are you doing, my friend?"

Tim nodded. "Fine. It's beautiful here, really. Your country, your people, so warm, welcoming."

"But?"

Tim tossed sand through his fingers. "It's not the same, I guess. It's hard to explain. You wouldn't understand. It's like sex after a vasectomy. It's still good, but there's just something missing."

"You are right. I do not understand."

"Why would you?" Tim said. "You see, it's like—have you ever eaten a seedless watermelon?" Nino looked confused. Tim explained, "They make seedless watermelons, no pits, artificially grown. They taste good, but there's something missing. You can't put your finger on it, but there's something missing."

Nino took a deep breath. It was time. "Tim, I must tell you news from America. It is not good news."

Upon hearing it, Tim clutched his chest in anguish. His sobs were guttural; tears puddled onto the sand. "What have I done?"

"It wasn't you, or anything you did, or even could have done to prevent it. He had some illness I don't quite understand. A rare disease named after a—how do you say?—ball player. *Zio* said you'd recognize it." He explained more details as best he could. Tim sniffled, cried, and shook his head.

"I knew something, I knew something was wrong. Oh, my God, my God. But for him to do that. He must have felt hopeless, alone. If I was there . . ."

"No, nothing would have changed," Nino said.

"Your uncle and Frankie, how did they deal with this? I should have been there for them. Oh, my God. I've got to go back. Frankie had to handle the funeral arrangements. Oh, my God, how did he get through that? I've got to go home. He's got to be hurting. He could hardly say goodbye to me, and I was living. I've got to go home."

"Tim!"

"I must find a way, Nino," Tim insisted.

Nino sipped his wine and thought. "Do you trust me?" he asked.

"Of course, I do."

"Then you must do as I say. I promised my uncle I'd watch you. You are my responsibility."

❋

Chapter LII

It *wasn't until late spring* that the inscription was placed on the Odelli stone at Frankie's direction. Frankie and Johnny stood at the foot of the grave, staring at the headstone.

Claudio Odelli, MD
1953–2018

They bowed their heads. "I can't believe he's dead," Johnny said. "Cardio, gone."

Frankie nodded. "How well did you know him?" Frankie asked.

Johnny looked at him, confused by the question. "I don't know, 40 years, maybe more. Why do you ask?"

Frankie shook his head. "I asked how well, not how long." Johnny raised his eyebrows. "Forget it," Frankie said. "I was just asking—no reason." They turned to leave. "I'm so pissed at him," Frankie said. "I curse him for what he did to himself."

Frankie was not handling this well. He asked the same questions he'd been asking since the doctor's death. *How could he? What did we miss? How could we not know? Why didn't you tell us, you son of a bitch?* Frankie understood the five stages of grief; he realized that, even after months, he was still stuck on stage one, denial.

Johnny had no answers, either. "We were all wrapped up with Tim," Johnny said. "It's not like we could have done anything."

"We could have been there. We could have shown him that he wasn't alone through this. That he didn't have to do this."

"Frankie, he was his own man, a smart man. He knew what his future had in store and made this decision, like he said in the letter. He chose to go out on his own terms. You've got to stop blaming yourself. I missed it, too. He was our closest friend. He could have convinced us to help him do it. *That* would have been a *real* dilemma."

Frankie did not answer. He recognized his own state of depression. A lifetime of caregiving, of grief and tears had taken its toll. He was burnt out. It was caregiver's fatigue, a type of post-traumatic stress disorder. He had been intimately acquainted with death for half a century and had no answers, only questions. In search of answers, he visited Cardio's office. The building's superintendent was watering newly planted flowers.

"Excuse me," he said. "I wonder if you can help me. I'm Frankie Grace." The man put the hose down and wiped his hands on his coveralls. "Yes, Mr. Grace. I've been to your place many times. How can I help you?"

"I was wondering if I might be able to look into Dr. Odelli's office?"

The man cocked his head. "Odelli's office," the man repeated. "Well, I guess it would be no harm. Don't know what you hope to see. It hasn't been touched since his . . ." The words faded. "Anyway, follow me."

Frankie followed him to Odelli's office. The man fumbled through a keychain, finally finding the one to open the door. Frankie walked into a small reception area. Rockwell prints adorned the wall.

"Everything is the same as the day he left," the man said.

"You were here that day?" Frankie asked.

"Sure was. I helped him pack." Frankie walked around, not knowing what he hoped to find. The exam room was empty but for an exam table. The cabinets were bare, no instruments, the trash can empty. Frankie felt a chill as he stood by the door. He was trying to channel his friend, trying to put himself in Cardio's shoes, to think what he thought. He walked to the desk and saw the wheelchair.

"How long had he been using this?" he asked.

"Oh, I'd say a year or so. I brought it up to him when it was delivered. He was having trouble walking. He used a cane, and then two canes, and then this. He said the chair would help him rest his legs. Toward the end, he could hardly stand up."

Frankie sat in the wheelchair and surveyed the room. He tried to put himself in Cardio's mind, to think what he was thinking. The empty frames, the open safe, and empty file cabinet all added up to planning—long-term planning.

"Looks like he emptied everything," Frankie observed.

"Yes," the man said. "I helped him that day. I helped him take boxes to his car. He said he was retiring. I even mailed the letters to his patients. I told him he deserved to enjoy himself. Then—well, you know."

Frankie remembered carrying those boxes. As he thought about it now, he concluded that Cardio had piggybacked on their plan to pursue his own plan. While he was still in charge and able, Cardio would choose the time and place. Not trusting his friends with his torment, though, was an unforgivable offense that Frankie couldn't accept.

Back at the restaurant, Frankie was sitting by himself, reading the note over and over again. Cardio began his note with an apology. "Dear Frankie, I am deeply sorry to put you through this. I wish there were another way. I know it is selfish of me to expect this of you, but knowing you will be there for me is a comfort. Knowing you will understand my actions." He banged his hand on the bar. "You were wrong—you were wrong. I don't understand." He remembered Cardio's eulogy. Was there a message there that he missed? *Remember the good; judge the good.*

Day after day, Frankie left the funeral home earlier and earlier and returned later and later. He couldn't be there anymore. The walls were closing in. He went through the days in a mental fog, unable to help others through their grief, unable to face his. The very business that had given him everything he had, took everything he had; it zapped his spirit, pilfered his soul, leaving him emotionally drained.

He'd sit alone at the bar, drinking more than eating, reading the note over and over, shaking his head in disbelief. Paradise's Italian Restaurant was where he needed to be. He needed this connection. He hoped the memories of the laughter would drown out the ghosts. He recognized the mask he'd been wearing his whole life. His desire to laugh, to enjoy friends, to live to excess was a direct result of the task he was called upon to perform each day. He was letting himself go now. He had nothing left to give.

"Marco," Frankie called out, "espresso and another cognac." It was late. Johnny had just thanked the last couple, who'd spent an inordinate amount of time sharing a *tartufo* off each other's tongue. *Get a room, for God's sake,* Johnny thought. Frankie was sitting in a corner booth. He had dozed off but woke to order another drink. Marco looked at Johnny for instructions.

"Bring the espresso," he said, "a double. Eighty-six on the booze." He walked over, slid in next to his friend, and put his arm around his shoulder. "Frankie, my friend, it's late. You have to work tomorrow. You have a funeral."

Frankie picked his head off his chest and gripped the table with both hands. "I'm fine."

"I know. I know you're fine. But you need to get some rest. You have work in the morning. You have to go home, sleep."

Frankie looked at him, his words slightly slurred. "Nooo, I can't go home. Ghosts," he explained.

Johnny raised his eyebrows. "Ghosts?"

Frankie nodded. "I see ghosts, spirits all around me. I hear people crying, mourners; mothers for their children, children for their moms. I don't want to go to work anymore. I can't do it. I can't. I buried my mother, father, uncles, cousins, friends, best friends. Everyone I love. It's not fair, not normal, but that's what I do, and I can't do it anymore. They're haunting me now."

Marco brought espresso to the table—one for Johnny, too. "Frankie, you're an undertaker, a funeral director. People depend on you. You help people. That is what you do. That is who you are."

"No!" Frankie stopped him. A small smile came across his face. "I'm not. I'm a comic, a clown." He picked up a spoon, rubbed it, and placed it on his nose. "You see, watch." The spoon fell to the table. "Needs work," he said.

Johnny slid the cup closer to Frankie. "Frankie, what you do is special. You have a calling. It's a tough job, I know. Not everyone can do it. I hear people talking at funeral luncheons about the funeral, how beautiful, meaningful it was. You make that possible. You're not cookie-cutter. You make a difference. God made you for this." .

"Screw Him, too, then. I didn't want this." He tried again to attach the spoon to his nose.

"I'll tell you what I know. People depend on you, trust you to care for their dead. You're Frankie Grace."

Frankie slid out of the booth. "No," he said, "I'm a comic, a clown. I'm Pagliacci. Ha, ha, ha, ha." With that, he staggered out of the restaurant.

"Follow him home," Johnny said. Marco nodded.

Johnny tapped his fingers on the table. He called his nephew. "No tie, a five o'clock shadow, it's not like him. He comes to the restaurant earlier and earlier," he explained. "He's here so early, he signs for deliveries. He's the last to leave at night. He's losing it. I'm worried about him."

"Be patient, *zio*."

✲

Chapter LIII

*J*ohnny *was changing burnt-out bulbs* on the Christmas lights. Sinatra was singing "I'll Be Home for Christmas," D-15 on the juke box. Frankie had dozed off, slumped in a booth at the restaurant. When he opened his eyes, he saw Johnny at the bar in conversation with another man. He wiped away a veil of sleep and focused. He still had a buzz from his liquid lunch. He heard the man talking as Johnny flipped through pages of a ledger. There was something familiar about the distant voice, something familiar about the figure itself. He wiped his face with a napkin and took stock of himself. The man was dressed in a blue sports jacket, gray pants, with a red knit scarf around his neck. The outfit looked familiar. Then he focused on the man's shoes. Black suede, Bruno Magli. He watched the man's movements, all very familiar, his arm gesticulating and that voice. Suddenly, a ringtone danced off the man's phone, "Volare." "*Pronto,*" he answered.

Frankie walked toward the stranger, step by step. Johnny nodded, and the man turned around. They were face to face. Frankie stared at him, examining, seeing but not seeing, confused, disoriented. But for a mustache, and a full head of hair and perfect teeth, the man looked familiar. He looked beyond the mustache, beyond the aquiline nose, behind tinted eyeglasses, and into bright blue eyes. He thought he was hallucinating. "Tim? Tim? Is that you?"

A beaming smile came over Tim's face. "Hello, my brother from another mother. How the hell are you?" The two men embraced, as Johnny wiped a tear from his eye and honked his nose. Frankie stepped back to examine the face again. He squeezed Tim's nose and tugged on a strand of hair.

"Is it you? How, how?"

"You think I'd let my friends go through this alone?"

"But, how?" He was staring at a new man.

Tim pointed to Johnny. "His nephew, like Dr. Frankenstein. He made me a new man, literally. Kid's pretty bright. The Sciacca clinic was amazing. Nino had me running every day. I lost 40 pounds." He opened his jacket to show off his waistline. "He was like a gestapo," he continued. "I swam in the Mediterranean. They got these special thermal springs from some saint or other. He'd hook me up to a centrifuge, took my blood, mixed it with ozone, and put it back into me intravenously. It was like being embalmed but while I was still living. You see, it's all about the platelets. Anyway, the kid's sharp. They injected me with zinc. Needles, right into my scalp—that's what grew this. Man, did that hurt. The things I do for you guys. It's real. Go ahead, pull it again. A periodontist gave me a new smile, a plastic surgeon tucked in the crow's feet and pulled up my chin, contacts made my eyes blue—and the biggest thing," he pointed to his nose, "look at this *schnozzola*. It's normal size now."

"Major surgery," Johnny observed. Tim raised his middle finger. Proof positive for Frankie.

"But, but how can you come back? If they find you, you're dead."

"Not to worry. I'm hiding in plain sight. Johnny needs help running this place. Business has tripled since the shooting. Thanks to me. We worked it out."

"You knew about this?" he asked Johnny.

Johnny blew his nose again. "We wanted to surprise you."

"By the way, I'm not Luciano Greco anymore. Go figure. I just got used to Luciano." He showed Frankie his license. "Robert Reynolds—a bit pedestrian, waspy, but hey, it was the best I could get from the Camorra. Hey, did you know there's a mafia there, too? They're like AT&T, all connected."

Frankie was dizzy. He fell back onto a barstool. "You can't stay here. Sam eats here all the time."

"Hey, don't worry. I'm sure he's not pissed anymore." He pointed to Johnny. "This guy's cousin Sebastiano interceded on my behalf. He sent people to meet Sam. I made a deal. My lawyer settled all my debts with my life-insurance money. I paid everyone back. And, Sam's case got thrown out because, without me, there was no case. So, he's happy. I'm turning a new leaf. I bet you I never place another bet."

"Holy moly," Frankie said. "You scammed the insurance company."

"Not really," Tim said. "I took an advance out on my life insurance. They'd have to pay someday. What's the difference now or twenty years from now? Tracy left town with her share. In the end, I couldn't stiff her. I hear she went to South America. It's all good. Marco," he called out, "give us your best bottle of cheap wine. Hey, where's Marco?"

Johnny's eyebrows rose high above his head. "Uh, Marco quit. He went back home to Ecuador."

"Hey, what a coincidence. I think that's where Tracy . . ." He stopped mid-sentence.

"They got chummy at your funeral luncheon," Johnny explained, apologetically, "after all you were dead."

"Why, that two-timing *Puttana*! I wasn't even cold. And Marco, he's got my wife and $200K from my insurance. They'll live like kings."

Frankie rubbed his eyes.

"So, tell me, how did my funeral go after I left? Were there a lot of people crying? How was the lunch?"

Frankie was dazed, half expecting to be awakened from a dream.

"Frankie," Tim said; his tone had become somber. He'd avoided the subject until now. "Are you okay? Are you okay, my friend?"

Frankie nodded. "I will be. Have no choice, do I?"

"I went to the cemetery yesterday," Tim said. "It's impossible to get my head around it. I don't know how you got through it. I'm sorry I wasn't here for him. Sorry I wasn't here for you guys."

"It wouldn't have changed. We were here and didn't see, couldn't see, couldn't help. I'll never forgive him. Never," Frankie said.

"You have to walk in a man's shoes," Johnny said. "Those were his words, remember? You gotta be lucky to get out of this world alive. Without debilitating pain, or sickness, disease. We can only hope to die in our sleep. That's what he meant."

"Remember what he said at my funeral?" Tim added. "Remember the good; don't judge."

"How would you know that?" Frankie asked.

Tim looked down, "I made a stop before the airport. I couldn't miss it. It's a once-in-a-lifetime opportunity to see your own funeral." Frankie shook his head. "Hey, a toast," Tim proposed. "To Cardio."

Under the watchful eyes and pierced velvet canvas of Johnny Paradise, Sr., the three men lifted a glass. "To Cardio!"

"To Cardio."

"To Cardio."

❋

Chapter LIV

*F*rankie was doing paperwork when Gregoria called. "Frankie, I need your help again."

"Another indigent?" Frankie asked.

"No, no. I need you to amend a death certificate. Remember Jane Doe?"

"Yes, of course. I already amended her death certificate to Mathilda Todd."

"Well," he said, "we have to do it again."

Frankie leaned back. "I'm confused," he said.

"Understandable," Gregoria answered. "Have you ever heard of the Innocence Project?"

Frankie thought for a moment. "Can't say I have," he said.

"A group of law students who work to overturn convictions based on new DNA or other evidence. A pretty impressive record, I must say."

Frankie was lost. "Okay?" was all he could muster.

"Anyway, it seems Jane Doe, AKA Mathilda Todd, was actually Shirly Chesapeak. We found a letter she wrote to her niece. She never mailed it. We tracked her down. Seems her niece became a lawyer and dedicated her life to proving her aunt's innocence. She worked for this Innocence Project and as fate would have it she got her aunt's conviction overturned.

Frankie repeated the name, "'Shirly Chesapeak'? Should that mean anything to me?"

"No, not at all. Seems Shirly was convicted in 1978 of a bank robbery in which a guard was killed. She maintained her innocence but was convicted and sentenced to life in prison."

"I'm sorry, Mr. Gregoria. I'm not following you."

"Chesapeak escaped while en route to prison. She's been on the run for more than 40 years. She evaded authorities, living under the radar, under assumed identities, the last one being 'Mathilda Todd.'"

"Jesus! Are you saying 'Mathilda Todd' was an alias?"

"Exactly. One of many, I'd imagine," Gregoria said. "She was featured no less than six times on *America's Most Wanted* but to no avail. When her niece was finally interviewed, the whole thing came to light."

"But . . ."

Yep, the niece never gave up. Shirly Chesapeak's verdict was overturned a year ago. The Innocence Project won a major victory, examining her DNA with today's new technology. Isn't science wonderful? Turns out, she didn't do it. She spent a lifetime on the run, different towns and aliases. Jane Doe AKA Mathilda Todd is actually Shirly Chesapeak. That's why she was found with no identification at a bus stop. She must have been on the move for some reason. Unfortunately, she probably never knew she had been vindicated. What do you make of that?"

Frankie's throat was dry. "It's incredible."

"I'll say. Anyway, I'll fax you all we know. Please amend the certificate. Have you ever had anything like this—false identities, assumed names?"

Frankie took a deep breath. "Can't say I have. It reminds me of an old friend who once asked me, 'At the end of the day, does anyone ever know anyone?'"

"Guess not," Gregoria answered. "Take care of that for me, and send an updated certificate and all paperwork to her niece."

"Will do," Frankie said. He felt a tinge of satisfaction. If only Shirly knew that she helped get one over on the feds. She might just feel good about that.

⚹

Epilogue

Even after receiving the medal for Meritorious Achievement, awarded by the FBI for exceptional and extraordinary service, Reno Amore felt empty. For all the cases he'd solved, his days and nights were spent wondering about the case of Timothy Collins. It kept him up at night, twisting and turning, fighting in his sheets. Sleep was elusive—like a spoiled fisherman not content with the fish he'd caught but consumed with the ones that got away. He knew he had been played but couldn't put the pieces together. Knowing there were four people who knew they had gotten over on him depressed him even more. His case against Sam Napoli and others collapsed with the death of his inside informant, Tim Collins. It made retirement on Long Beach Island less than fulfilling.

As he sipped iced coffee on a veranda, an article in the *New York Times* caught his eye. The FBI had cleared a cold case because of the work of the Innocence Project. The conviction against Shirly Chesapeak had been overturned unanimously by an Appellate Court, posthumously, it would seem. The Innocence Project had introduced new DNA evidence. She had been convicted in 1978 of bank robbery and murder during a robbery. She was sentenced to life in prison and escaped en route to the federal penitentiary when the vehicle transporting her was in an accident. Amore knew the case well. Her career on the run had mirrored his rise in the agency. The article explained that Chesapeak went into hiding and successfully evaded capture. She lived under assumed names and false identities. Even being featured countless times on *America's Most Wanted* proved fruitless. A great-grandniece received regular communication over the years with no return address. "She ended each letter proclaiming her innocence," her niece stated. *The Times* reported, "Chesapeak's last known identity was Mathilda Todd. She'd lived under the radar in the hamlet of Inlet Cove in Westchester, New York, for 15 years. She'd worked as a domestic before winding up in a senior facility, as far as authorities could piece together." Mathilda's body had been found at a bus stop in Inlet Cove on December 9, 2017. She died from hypothermia. She was most likely unaware that her conviction had been overturned. Shirly was cremated and her ashes interred at a local cemetery. The niece revealed that she was first informed of her aunt's death by the county's public administrator under the name "Mathilda Todd." The niece was quoted as saying, "My aunt spent a lifetime on the run for a crime she did not commit. She lived a solitary life looking over her shoulder and died alone, left rotting in a morgue for months as Jane Doe. I was notified by a benevolent funeral director who claimed her body that she was cremated on February 20, months after her death. I thank Mr. Grace for that."

Amore put the paper down. He didn't believe in coincidence. He read the date of Chesapeak's death and cremation again and again. Then, enlightenment! "I'll be damned," he said. "Those bastards. Those clever, sneaky, dirty bastards."

~ The End ~

Acknowledgments

Some of the precious few people who read my first book, *Die Laughing,* have, on occasion, asked me, "What ever happened to Frankie Grace?" *The Romeo Club* answers that question. Frankie is much older. He relocated to Westchester, made a new life with new friends but never forgot his old ones. I chose to self-publish The Romeo Club because I understand I am too old to be "discovered" by a literary agent. I'd like to thank Michelle DeFilippo and Ronda Rawlins at 1106 Design for their patience, guidance and expertise in moving the book forward. On a personal note and at this particular time in my life, I'd like to thank the Jimmys and Joes, the Henrys and Moes, Mikes, Ikes, the Frankies, Toms, and Doms, Dannys and Rons, Ralphies, Bobs, Tonys and Robs, and all who have been charter members of my own Romeo Club over the years. Remember, live large, tip well.

About the Author

Vincent Graziano is the married father of two children and grand-father of three. He is a product of Manhattan's iconic Little Italy. The life experiences he had as a young man growing up on those city streets have shaped him and are evident in his writing. After a failed attempt as a stand-up comic, he continued his studies and graduated Pace University. He is a licensed funeral director, still active in the funeral profession with his children, with locations in Westchester, NY, and Greenwich, CT. To contact him, email him at v.graziano53@gmail.com

Made in the USA
Coppell, TX
14 May 2022

77787138R00152